THIS IS
LONDON

WITNESSES TO WAR

THIS IS LONDON

EDWARD R. MURROW

EDITED WITH AN
INTRODUCTION, COMMENTARY,
AND FOOTNOTES
BY
ELMER DAVIS

SCHOCKEN BOOKS / NEW YORK

Copyright 1941 by Edward R. Murrow
Copyright renewed 1969 by Janet H. B. Murrow and
Charles Casey Murrow

All rights reserved under International and Pan-American
Copyright Conventions. Published in the United States by
Schocken Books Inc., New York. Distributed by Pantheon
Books, a division of Random House, Inc., New York.
Originally published by Simon and Schuster, Inc., in 1941.

Library of Congress Cataloging-in-Publication Data

Murrow, Edward R.
This is London.

(Witnesses to war)
Reprint. Originally published: New York:
Simon and Schuster, 1941.
1. World War, 1939–1945—Great Britain—London.
2. World War, 1939–1945—Great Britain.
3. World War, 1939–1945.
4. World War, 1939–1945—Personal
narratives, American. 5. London (England)—History.
6. Great Britain—History—George VI, 1932–1952.
I. Title. II. Series.
D760.8.L7M8 1989   940.54′21   88-43245
ISBN 0-805-20882-8

The quotation on the back cover from *Murrow: His Life
and Times* by A. M. Sperber is reprinted by permission of
William Morris Agency, Inc., on behalf of the author.
Copyright © 1985.

Manufactured in the United States of America

Display Typography by
Eric Baker Design/Susi Oberhelman

First Schocken Books Edition

CONTENTS

INTRODUCTION

Everyone who listens to the war news is familiar with Ed Murrow's salutation, "This is London." That is what this book is about. From his broadcasts in the first sixteen months of the war these selections have been compiled, not as a day-by-day history, but in the belief that this is London —a record of what London thought and felt about a war that began as something remote and hardly real and gradually became the dominant reality of daily, and still more of nightly, life.

The selection has been made by F. W. Mordaunt Hall of the Columbia Broadcasting System's staff, and all those concerned with the production of the book applaud his choice. Yet it should be pointed out that Murrow himself might have made a different selection. The emphasis is perhaps not quite the same on the spot as at a distance; but Murrow had other things to think about, and this seems the best that could be done three thousand miles away. The reader might remember, too, that this is the language of speech, not of the printed page; all this material was designed to be heard, not read. But it is what Ed Murrow, and no one else, thought was what ought to be heard on any given date; as is explained in one of these broadcasts, the censorship under which he works is negative; it can tell him what to leave out but it never tries to tell him what to put in. And he talks under no instructions from the home office in New York except to find the news and report it.

We who work with Murrow are keenly aware of his excellence as a reporter of pure news; indeed some of us—having, like most radio news men, learned our trade in another medium—are perhaps faintly scandalized that such good reporting can be done by a man who never worked on a newspaper in his life, and acquired his basic experience of Europe first as president of the National Student Federation of the United States and then in the service of the Institute of International Education. The only objection that can be offered to Murrow's technique of reporting is that when an air raid is on he has the habit of going up on the roof to see what is happening, or of driving around town in an open car to see what has been hit. That is a good way to get the news, but perhaps not the best way to make sure that you will go on getting it.

But news is no longer news by the time it could be printed in a book, which explains some omissions in this volume. If you want to know what Murrow had to say in certain critical periods—the first few days after the signing of the German-Russian treaty, the first few days of the Blitzkrieg in the west, and so on—you will not find it here; for on those days his broadcasts were a chronicle of events which now are history. In this compilation news has been included only if it had some ironic value or some direct bearing on the states of mind which Murrow was reporting.

For this is the unique value of his broadcasts—their reflection of the changing ideas and emotions, the hopes and the fears and the endeavors to look ahead, of Englishmen of nearly all classes, high and low. No one yet knows *whether there will be a Europe fit to live in after this war; but if there is, it will be due chiefly to such Englishmen as those whose thoughts and feelings are recorded here—men who even in the stress of the struggle for survival find time occasionally to look ahead, to try to make up their minds what they want and what they may have some hope of getting if they win. It is, you may observe, a very different England (or Britain, if particularistic Scots insist on the distinction) from the Britain which was one of the characters in the drama of prewar international politics. That difference is the most hopeful thing about it.*

ELMER DAVIS

February, 1941
New York

THIS IS LONDON

August 19 to September 28, 1939

AUGUST 19, 1939. *The Soviet Union signs a trade agreement with Germany embracing a German credit of 200,000,000 marks and a Soviet undertaking to purchase goods valued at 180,000,000 marks from Germany.*

AUGUST 21. *With British and French military missions still in Moscow, the German government announces that the Russo-German trade agreement is to be followed by a ten-year nonaggression pact.*

AUGUST 22. *The British Cabinet officially announces that the Nazi-Soviet pact will not affect the British pledge to guarantee Poland against aggression.*

AUGUST 28. *France closes the German frontier.*

AUGUST 30. *The British Cabinet for a second time urges Hitler to negotiate directly with Poland. Hitler then claims no Polish representative appeared and presents Germany's demands to the British Ambassador in Berlin. These include: immediate return of Danzig to the Reich, a plebiscite in the Polish Corridor, a guarantee of the port of Gdynia to Poland, and free access by Germany to East Prussia.*

SEPTEMBER 1. *Germany sends troops across the Polish border. The Polish government calls for British and French support. The British and French governments send an ultimatum to Hitler announcing they will aid Poland unless German forces are withdrawn.*

SEPTEMBER 3. *Prime Minister Neville Chamberlain announces that a state of war with Germany began to exist at 11 A.M. France declares war that afternoon. Anthony Eden becomes*

1

Secretary of the Dominions. Winston Churchill becomes First Lord of the Admiralty.

SEPTEMBER 5.   German troops shell Warsaw and gain control of Upper Silesia. British planes drop 3,000,000 anti-Hitler circulars in Germany. President Roosevelt invokes the Neutrality Act.

SEPTEMBER 6.   German armies seize Cracow. French troops penetrate German territory near Swiss frontier.

SEPTEMBER 8.   President Roosevelt proclaims a national emergency "to the extent necessary for the proper observance, safeguarding, and enforcing of the neutrality of the United States and the strengthening of our national defense within the limits of peacetime authorizations."

SEPTEMBER 14.   The Polish Ambassador to Britain pleads for more effective aid as German troops advance rapidly on all Polish fronts and surround Warsaw.

SEPTEMBER 15.   The Soviet Union and Japan agree to an armistice in the fighting that has been in progress along the frontier of Manchukuo and Outer Mongolia since May 11.

SEPTEMBER 18.   German and Russian troops meet at Brest-Litovsk.

SEPTEMBER 28.   Soviet Premier Molotov and German Foreign Minister von Ribbentrop sign an agreement in Moscow partitioning Poland and signalizing the "disintegration of the Polish state."

WAR—BUT ONLY IN POLAND

[At midnight on August 21, 1939, it was announced in Berlin that Foreign Minister von Ribbentrop was going to Moscow to conclude a nonaggression treaty—or pact, as the headline writers like to call it—with Russia. This reversal of what the world had regarded as the two basic premises of international politics, Hitler's anti-Bolshevism and Stalin's anti-Nazism, was the lighting of the fuse. For the next few days Murrow, like all other radio and newspaper correspondents, was busy getting the news; and it might be recalled that he was the only American correspondent who gave due emphasis to the report of the Conservative party organization to Mr. Chamberlain. That report informed the Prime Minister, after a sampling of opinion, that the party was behind him in a policy of firmness; with the clear implication that it would not support him in a different policy. From the moment Ed Murrow put that on the air, some of us were convinced that there would be war. We begin these reports from the dispatch of the second British note, which included the remark that the Poles were willing to enter into discussions—a phrase erroneously interpreted in Berlin as meaning that they were ready to sign on the dotted line, as the Czechs had been compelled to do at Munich a year before. But in the interval Chamberlain had seen the light, or some of it.]

3

AUGUST 28, 1939

I have a feeling that Englishmen are a little proud of themselves tonight. They believe that their government's reply was pretty tough, that the Lion has turned and that the retreat from Manchukuo, Abyssinia, Spain and Czechoslovakia and Austria has stopped. They are amazingly calm; they still employ understatement, and they are inclined to discuss the prospects of war with, oh, a casual "bad show," or, "If this is peace, give me a good war." I have heard no one say as many said last September, "I hope Mr. Chamberlain can find a way out."

There is not much thinking going on over here. People seem to revert to habit in times likes this. Nothing seems to shake them. They lose the ability to feel. For instance, we had pictures in today's papers, pictures of school children carrying out a test evacuation. For them it was an adventure. We saw pictures of them tying on each other's identification tags, and they trooped out of the school building as though they were going to a picnic, and for them it was an adventure.

There is a feeling here that if Hitler does not back down he will probably move against the Poles—not the French and British in the first instance. Then the decision must be made here and in France, and a terrible decision it will be. I will put it to you with the brutal frankness with which it was put to me by a British politician this afternoon: "Are we to be the first to bomb women and children?"

The military timetable has certainly been drawn up, but so far as we know in London the train for an unknown destination hasn't started. Within the last two hours, I have talked to men who have a certain amount of firsthand information as to the state of mind in Whitehall and I may tell you that they see little chance of preserving peace. They feel that Herr Hitler may modify the demands, that the Italians may counsel against war, but they don't see a great deal of hope, and there the matter stands and there it may stand until Parliament meets tomorrow in that small, ill-ventilated room where so many decisions have been made. I shall be there to report it to you.

Well, if it is to be war, how will it end? That is a question Englishmen are asking, and for what will it be fought and what will be the position of the U. S. Of course, that is a matter for you to decide and you will reach your own conclusions in the light of more information than is available in any other country, and I am not going to talk about it. But I do venture to suggest that you watch carefully these moves during the next few days, that you further sift the evidence for what you will decide will be important, and there is more than enough evidence that the machinery to influence your thinking and your decisions has already been set up in many countries. And now, the last word that has reached London concerning tonight's development is that at the British Embassy in Berlin all the luggage of the personnel and staff has been piled up in the hall and it is remarked here that the most prominent article in the heavy luggage was a folded umbrella, given pride of placement amongst all the other pieces of baggage.

AUGUST 31, 1939—11 A.M.

All hours are given in New York time. London is five

hours later; that is, eleven in the morning in New York is four in the afternoon in London.

There are two pieces of information here in London, the first is that the Stock Exchange is to be closed tomorrow and the second has to do with the evacuation. Can't you imagine for a moment that you are a member of a family living perhaps in Battersea? Here is what you would have heard in a broadcast just a short while ago, presented very calmly in a well-modulated English voice. It has been decided to start evacuation of school children and other priority classes as already arranged under the government scheme, tomorrow, Friday, September 1. Poland should conclude from this decision that war is being regarded as inevitable. Evacuation which will take several days to complete is being taken as a precautionary measure in view of the prolongation of the period of tension. The government has been assured that the attitude of quiet confidence which the public have been displaying will continue. There are no elements which would interfere with the operation of the transport arrangements that are to take place and that all concerned in receiving areas will put aside every consideration of personal interest and convenience and do everything possible to contribute to the success of the great national undertaking. There then follows a long list of areas to be evacuated: Greater London and areas covered by the London County Council, towns such as Beckenham, Gravesend, Liverpool, Crosby, Manchester, Sheffield, and many others. The scheme applies to the following classes: children, children accompanied by their mothers or other responsible persons, blind persons and cripples whose removal is feasible. The plans are all ready for operation and they've been well rehearsed, but even though the arrangements may be familiar to those concerned, the directions which follow should be carefully noted.

In order that the process of evacuation may be carried out, all schools in evacuation and reception areas are to be closed for instruction from tomorrow, Friday morning, until further notice. This closure is for instructional purposes only. Then again we have a list of the areas to be evacuated.

Here now is a quotation from the official bulletin. If you live in one of the areas mentioned, or have a child of school age and wish to have him evacuated, you should send him to school tomorrow, Friday, with hand luggage containing the child's gas mask, a change of underclothing, night clothes, shoes, spare stockings or socks, a toothbrush, a comb, a towel, soap, face cloth, handkerchief, and if possible a warm coat or mackintosh. A packet of food for the day should also be included. School children will be taken by their teachers to homes in safer districts where they will be housed by people who have already offered to receive them and look after them. All parents of school children in these areas are strongly urged to let their children go. Parents will be told where their children are as soon as they reach their new home. The cost of the journey will be paid by the government. Parents who are in an evacuable area and do not wish their children to be evacuated should not send them to school until they are told to do so. Children of below school age can only be evacuated if their mothers or some other responsible person can go with them and look after them in the place to which they are sent, unless arrangements have been made to send them with a nursery school or day nursery.

Pasters are being distributed at the schools, showing the times, and mothers with children below school age should assemble at the school unless they have been notified in some other way. Mothers and others in charge of children below school age should take hand luggage with the same equipment for themselves as their children. As for school children, the names of the children should be written on strong paper and sewn onto their clothes. No one can take more than a little hand luggage. Mothers and others in charge of the children below school age will be provided with accommodations. For other respects they will have to make their own arrangements. Those who can should, therefore, take with them sufficient money to tide them over until they can get regular remittances from home, but no one should refrain from going merely because of difficulties in regard to money, as arrangements will be made to look after those who are in need. Arrangements are being made for the issuance of emergency rations. There will be sufficient food for forty-eight hours, so that purchases of food, other than minor purchases, need not be made in local shops during this period. It is asked that those who are included in this scheme should not accept accommodations in areas to which those evacuated will be sent.

There then follows in this official statement an announcement for people in Scotland. The official statement also states that there will be no evacuation in Wales. And the statement concludes by saying, during the evacuation period ordinary railway and road passenger services will be drastically reduced, liable to alteration at short notice.

It's too early to tell you with any degree of certainty the reaction of London to this announcement. A friend of mine who has just completed a tour of the city by cab tells me that so far as surface indications are concerned, one notices little difference between today and yesterday at this time.

Of course, it's useless to speculate concerning the reasons for this move in London today. You will remember that it was strongly advocated in the House of Commons on Tuesday; Mr. Arthur Greenwood, Deputy Leader of the Labour party, making a strong appeal at that time to the government to commence to act. Today it seems they feel unable longer to assume responsibility of keeping children and other categories in London.

AUGUST 31, 1939—3:15 P.M.

Last night the British reply was handed to the Germans. It was believed that a verbal answer was given but no official reply has yet been received in London. One London news agency reports from Berlin that Sir Nevile Henderson was told that negotiations between Britain and Germany were suspended. That report, however, is not confirmed here in London. The pessimists feel that we may never receive an official reply.* That remains to be seen. There is some indication that the nature of Germany's answer may be found in today's news in London. The Stock Exchange will be closed tomorrow. The reason given is that the evacuation of children and certain special categories of persons will interfere with business. Tomorrow we shall see the children, the halt, the lame, and the blind going out of Britain's

* They never did; except for Ribbentrop's midnight interview with Henderson, in which he recited at high speed the Sixteen Points, and then remarked that they were now out of date.

cities. Six hundred and fifty thousand will leave London tomorrow. The exodus will start at 5:30 in the morning. In
all there are three million people to be evacuated in the
crowded areas, one million three hundred thousand from
London alone. Nine roads out of London and only one-way
traffic. It's not going to be a very pleasant sight.

This afternoon we learned that the Navy had been fully
mobilized; all reservists have been called up for the Army
and the Royal Air Force had called up part of its reserves.
They are being called up by radio. There's none of the usual
business of individual notices. Now, this does not represent
complete mobilization, but it certainly calls up all the men
it can handle immediately. One thing incidentally: one evidence of the state of preparedness is that within two hours
after evacuation announcement was made, newspapers appeared in the streets with complete maps and detailed instructions for any who might care for them. Certain London taxis have been withdrawn from the streets, to be fitted
with special brackets to haul fire service trailers or pumps.
Women and children have been helping the men dig
trenches today. So far, Whitehall stands by its statement
that war is not regarded as inevitable. We in London know,
as you know, of the various diplomatic moves that have
gone on in Europe during the day. We know nothing of
their outcome, but the conviction has grown that we shall
have a decision before very long.

Those of you who are familiar with military terminology
will understand what I mean when I say that in London last
night the command seemed to be "stand steady." Tonight
it seems to be: "prepare for action."

SEPTEMBER 1, 1939

I should like to recapitulate a few things said from here on an earlier broadcast. First, that the British ultimatum without a time limit has been handed to von Ribbentrop, and it is believed that the communication will be discussed with Hitler before a reply is given. Second, that Poland has been hammered by the German military machine for nearly twenty-four hours, and the pledges of France and Britain which were to come into force at once have not become operative. Third, it has been expected in certain quarters that the Prime Minister would speak to the nation by radio tonight. He has not done so.

I also said that while delay yesterday and the day before might have been advantageous to the so-called peace front, delay today can hardly be helpful to the Poles and was not calculated to improve their morale. I reported those things. At the end of that broadcast you were told that my remarks might have created the impression that appeasement was in the air. I have said my say concerning appeasement. I reported that I have seen no evidences of it for some time. I have also given you such facts as are available in London tonight. I have an old-fashioned belief that Americans like to make up their own minds on the basis of all available information. The conclusions you draw are your own affair. I have no desire to influence them and shall leave such efforts to those who have more confidence in their own judgment than I have in mine.

Britain is not yet at war, but tomorrow morning's press speaks of war in the present tense. Here is the comment of the London *Times*. Last September, it was the first British newspaper to advocate the dismemberment of Czechoslovakia, and since that time it has consistently defended the policy embodied in the Munich agreement. Here is the quotation: "Since Herr Hitler has chosen war in spite of the many chances given to him up to the last hour to avoid it, war there must be." Then here is just one sentence from *The Times* which will give you some indication of the style of journalistic writing that still is employed, even at a time like this, in the newspaper that has been called "The Thunderer." Here is the sentence: "All the preparations made on the chance that the inhuman egotism of the ruler of Germany would rush blindly to catastrophe have proved adequate so far as they have yet been tested." In other words, *The Times* believes that so far Britain has done very well.

The Times concludes as follows: "The whole of the proceedings in Parliament yesterday were inspired by the conviction that a great evil must be erased from the world. That evil is the spirit of faithlessness, of intolerance, of bullying, and of senseless ambition which is embodied in Herr Hitler and those who surround him. The conviction overrides the horror of the thought that civilized man has had to tackle the same task twice in twenty-five years. The task will be done again, no matter what the effort required, and it will be done this time in a way which will insure that our children will not have to repeat it."

In general, tomorrow morning's press is unanimous in its support of the government. You have been told of the hardening of public opinion here, the unity in the House of Commons, and the calm steadiness of the British public. You have been told that many expected a declaration of war tonight, and you have been told that there has been delay because a final appeal has been made to Herr Hitler to withdraw—an appeal which the Prime Minister has said he does not expect to succeed.

I suggest that it is hardly time to become impatient over the delayed outbreak of a war which may spread over the world like a dark stain of death and destruction. We shall have the answer soon enough. If war comes tomorrow or the next day, most folks here believe that it will be a long war, and it is the historical belief of Britishers that wars are won at the end, not at the beginning.

SEPTEMBER 2, 1939

This is London. The Cabinet met fifteen minutes ago and is still in session. Well, where stands Britain tonight? I think, but I'm not sure, that she stands where she did. You have heard the Prime Minister's speech today. For the second time this country has expected the declaration of war and for the second time it hasn't come. Britain is still at peace.

If reports received in London are reliable, Britain's ally, Poland, is being subjected to invasion on the modern scale. Britain has pledged in the most solemn terms to come to Poland's assistance at once. She hasn't done so. The Prime Minister implies, at least, that the reason for the delay is to be found in Paris.* He wants an immediate decision. He admits that the House of Commons is perturbed. And I may tell you that many young peers were bewildered after that speech. And you should also know that the French

* It was, as the French Yellow Book makes clear.

Ambassador called at Downing Street shortly after the Prime Minister's speech.

Mr. Archibald Sinclair, leader of the Liberal opposition, had this to say: "I believe the whole House is perturbed by the Prime Minister's statement. There is a growing feeling in the House, I believe in all quarters of the House, that this strain must end sooner or later, and in a sense, the sooner the better." And he went on to say: "I hope tomorrow, however hard the work may be for the Prime Minister, and no one would care to be in his shoes tonight, that we shall know the mind of the government. The moment that we look like weakening, at that moment the dictatorships know that we are beaten."

The military mission from Moscow has arrived in Berlin. We hear, from both London and Paris, friendly references to Mussolini. The stock market in Amsterdam, and a very sensitive market it is, is bullish today. It goes up to fifteen points. We hear all sorts of wild rumors, but one thing is certain. The House of Commons meets at noon tomorrow, and we shall then have a decision. The Prime Minister says that he has not yet received an answer to Britain's ultimatum to Germany. Will he have received one by tomorrow? I don't know, but unless I misjudge entirely the temper of this country, one of three things will have happened by one o'clock tomorrow afternoon. Either Britain will have honored her obligations to Poland and have declared war on Germany; or the Germans will have withdrawn within their own frontier; or some standstill agreement will have been reached through the mediation of Mussolini. The possibility even of a five-power conference is being discussed. Take your choice.

We saw today in the House of Commons the Left wing and Liberal group pressing for a decision.* There has been for some time a truce to party politics in this country, and it seems unlikely that any government can continue beyond noon tomorrow the policy expressed by the Prime Minister in the House this afternoon, without splitting this country from end to end.

There is nothing in Britain's pledge to Poland necessitating consultation with other allies. The Prime Minister spoke of the delay in negotiating with Britain's allies by telephone. It is true, of course, that this isn't simply a matter of declaring war. Decisions must be taken concerning the actual military measures to be undertaken. How, for instance, are Britain and France to bring help to the Poles? Are they to take the initiative in bombing of women and children? Well, this situation could not have come as a surprise to His Majesty's government. For months, staff conversations between the British and French have been going on. We have been told repeatedly that there is complete solidarity between Britain and France. And yet, I have been told tonight that the delays are occasioned by military, rather than by political, reasons.

Some people have told me tonight that they believe a big deal is being cooked up which will make Munich and the betrayal of Czechoslovakia look like a pleasant tea party. I find it difficult to accept this thesis. I don't know what's in the mind of the government, but I do know that to Britishers their pledged word is important, and I should be very

* This was the day when the leader of the Labour opposition, rising in a House two-thirds Conservative, was greeted with the appeal, "Speak for England!"

much surprised to see any government which betrayed that pledge remain long in office. And it would be equally surprising to see any settlement achieved through the mediation of Mussolini produce anything other than a temporary relaxation of the tension.

Most observers here agree that this country is not in the mood to accept a temporary solution. And that's why I believe that Britain in the end of the day will stand where she is pledged to stand, by the side of Poland in a war that is now in progress. Failure to do so might produce results in this country, the end of which cannot be foreseen. Anyone who knows this little island will agree that things happen slowly here; most of you will agree that the British during the past few weeks have done everything possible in order to put the record straight. When historians come to sum up the last six months of Europe's existence, when they come to write the story of the origins of the war, or of the collapse of democracy, they will have many documents from which to work. As I said, I have no way of ascertaining the real reason for the delay, nor am I impatient for the outbreak of war.

What exactly determined the government's decision is yet to be learned. What prospects of peaceful solution the government may see is to me a mystery. You know their record. You know what action they've taken in the past, but on this occasion the little man in the bowler hat, the clerks, the bus drivers, and all the others who make up the so-called rank and file would be reckoned with. They seem to believe that they have been patient, that they have suffered insult and injury, and they certainly believe that this time they are going to solve this matter in some sort of permanent fashion. Don't think for a moment that these people here aren't conscious of what's going on, aren't sensitive to the suspicions which the delay of their government has aroused. They're a patient people, and they're perhaps prepared to wait until tomorrow for the definite word. If that word means war, the delay was not likely to have decreased the intensity or the effectiveness of Britain's effort. If it is peace, with the price being paid by Poland, this government will have to deal with the passion it has aroused during the past few weeks. If it's a five-power conference, well, we shall see.

The Prime Minister today was almost apologetic. He's a politician; he sensed the temper of the House and of the country. I have been able to find no sense of relief amongst the people with whom I've talked. On the contrary, the general attitude seems to be, "We are ready, let's quit this stalling and get on with it." As a result, I think that we'll have a decision before this time tomorrow. On the evidence produced so far, it would seem that that decision will be war. But those of us who've watched this story unroll at close range have lost the ability to be surprised.

SEPTEMBER 3, 1939

Forty-five minutes ago the Prime Minister stated that a state of war existed between Britain and Germany. Air-raid instructions were immediately broadcast, and almost directly following that broadcast the air-raid-warning siren screamed through the quiet calm of this Sabbath morning. There were planes in the sky. Whose, we couldn't be sure.* Now we're sitting quite comfortably underground. We're

* Their own, of course.

told that the "all-clear" signal has been sounded in the streets, but it's not yet been heard in this building.

In a few minutes we shall hope to go up into the sunlight and see what has happened. It may have been only a rehearsal. London may not have been the objective—and may have been.

I have just been informed that upstairs in the sunlight everything is normal; that cars are traveling through the streets, there are people walking in the streets and taxis are cruising about as usual.

The crowd outside Downing Street received the first news of war with a rousing cheer, and they heard that news through a radio in a car parked near Downing Street.

SEPTEMBER 4, 1939

At this time last night I ventured to suggest that this war might be fought in its early stages at least with pamphlets and radio, rather than with bombs. Tonight it is officially announced that "last night the Royal Air Force reconnoitered extensive areas of northern and western Germany. They flew unmolested and dropped six million leaflets in Germany." You will note that official communiqué said nothing about casualties. It states that they flew unmolested.

It is also announced that naval activities continue in all seas, but as yet there are no major operations to report. Official statements and press reports in London assume and indeed assert that the sinking of the *Athenia* was the work of Germany. So far as I know, no concrete proof has been produced: at least, it hasn't been published.

Sir John Anderson stated in the House this afternoon

that all aliens that might be hostile to this country must be rendered harmless. Just what that phrase "rendered harmless" means, I don't quite know, but a number of aliens are already under detention. All German and Austrian subjects over the age of sixteen must report to the police. Former citizens of Czechoslovakia are not to be treated as enemies.

A little more than three hours ago London had completed the removal of 600,000 people, without a single casualty.

The price of meat has been fixed by order. The price is not to be more than it was during the week ending August 25. It's also announced that the Ministry of Supply has assumed control of silk, flax, and aluminum.

For several days, I've reported, or repeated to you, calls for ambulance drivers, stretcher bearers, and personnel of the civilian defense. It might be useful to request the services of a good sociologist because if this business of repeated air alarms goes on the sociological results will be considerable. This is a class-conscious country. People live in the same small street or apartment building for years and never talk to each other. The man with a fine car, good clothes, and perhaps an unearned income doesn't generally fraternize with the tradesmen, day laborers, and truck drivers. His fences are always up. He doesn't meet them as equals. He's surrounded with certain evidences of worldly wealth, calculated to keep others at a distance, but if he's caught in Piccadilly Circus when a siren sounds, he may have a waitress stepping on his heels and see before him the broad back of a day laborer as he goes underground. If the alarm sounds about four in the morning, as it did this morning, his dignity, reserve, and authority may suffer when he arrives half dressed and sleepy, minus his usual defenses, and possessed of no more courage than those others who have arrived in similar state. Someone, I think it was Marcus Aurelius, said something to the effect that "death put Alexander of Macedon and his stable boy on a par." Repeated visits to public air-raid shelters might have produced the same results. Maybe I'm wrong, I'm not a very good sociologist, but I can tell you this from personal experience, that sirens would improve your knowledge of even your most intimate friend. London as usual is black tonight. One gets accustomed to it, but it can hardly be called pleasant. I don't know how you feel about the people who smoke cigarettes, but I like them, particularly at night in London. That small dull, red glow is a very welcome sight. It prevents collisions, makes it unnecessary to heave to, until you locate the exact position of those vague voices in the darkness. One night several years ago I walked bang into a cow, and since then i've had a desire for man and beast to carry running lights on dark nights. They can't do that in London these nights, but the cigarettes are a good substitute. For a moment tonight I thought I was back in the London of Mr. Pickwick's time. I heard a voice booming through the stark London streets. It said, "28 Courtland Place, all's well." It was an air-raid warden; he had shouted to someone an order to cover their window, they had done so, and so he was telling them that no more light came through.

SEPTEMBER 9, 1939

Three years of war. That's the estimate of the War Cabinet in London. That's the assumption—three years or more.

All departments are being instructed to prepare plans on this assumption. That statement is regarded here as irrefutable evidence that Great Britain is determined to see this war through to the end, no matter how long it may take.

Last night the Royal Air Force made its fifth pamphlet flight over Germany. On the return journey, Belgian planes engaged the British and from Brussels comes the news that the British Ambassador expressed deep regret and apology.

Effective tomorrow all chilled or frozen or freshly killed meat will be requisitioned by the government. Also, from tomorrow midnight all wholesale stocks of sugar, together with future arrivals, will be taken over by the government. Britain has issued no further word about fighting on the western front. But a survey of available reports indicates an absence of large-scale operations. Tonight the official bulletin from the Minister of Information says that enemy shipping is being swept from the seas. You all know about Marshal Goering's speech today—a brief but fair summary of it was broadcast in this country. Now here is the reaction of Reuter's diplomatic correspondent: "Field Marshal Goering's speech is regarded in well-informed quarters (that is, well-informed quarters here in London) as a strange mixture of braggadocio and reasonableness interspersed with occasional flashes of humor and marked by a certain note of moderation. It contains a strong appeal to Great Britain to reconsider her position and the whole position in the light of Germany's successes to date. But it is felt that he deliberately overlooked the power of resistance which makes the Polish army a factor still to be taken into account. The most significant part of this speech is his appeal to Mr. Chamberlain, with whom he says the issues of peace and

war still lie. His concern on the subject is deep and obviously genuine." Reuter's diplomatic correspondent adds
that the Germans would appear to be still hoping against
hope that the resolution of Great Britain and France to
fight Nazism to the bitter end is not irrevocable. But this
hope, it is emphatically declared, will prove in vain.

That statement, I think, can be taken as reflecting official
opinion here in London. I neglected to tell you one thing
about London. As a matter of fact, this particular aspect of
the war didn't hit me with full force until this afternoon—
Saturday afternoon over here. It's dull in London now that
the children are gone. For six days I've not heard a child's
voice. And that's a strange feeling. No youngsters shouting
their way home from school. And that's the way it is in
most of Europe's big cities now. One needs the eloquence
of the ancients to convey the full meaning of it. There just
aren't any more children.

Today I've learned some things about what's going on in
those empty homes. Most parents have now received letters
telling them that all is well. The children seem to be enjoy-
ing it. One mother of ten who still had five older children
at home said, "The house was deserted." She received a letter today from her child in the country and that mother
wanted to know the meaning of the word weaving.

I lunched today at the Savoy Grill. It was busy as usual;
in fact, a little better than usual. The place was crowded
with government officials, members of Parliament, a few
stranded Americans, and British and American correspondents. I met a man who is likely to become the best-hated
man in Germany. For he, or rather it is his job to starve
Germany by any known means, all of them, men, women,

and children. He is Director of the Ministry of Economic Warfare. His name is Sir Frederick Leith Ross. He is a quiet, unassuming man, almost shy. He is said to have one of the best financial minds in Europe. His is an important ministry. He is expected to do a good job of it. Few people, I think, will envy him this time. Sir Frederick seemed to be just a courteous, intelligent Britisher, with a job of work to do. We didn't discuss his job or his personal feelings about it.

Now here's one item that was given at the end of tonight's news broadcast. Motorists who claim in the future to have seen zebras in the forests should not be disbelieved. The New Forest Common Earth Defense Association advocated today that wild ponies should have white stripes painted on them so that they may be more easily seen by motorists in blackouts.

And that's London at 11:45, all quiet and all calm.

October 14, 1939, to April 7, 1940

OCTOBER 14, 1939. *The British Admiralty announces the torpedoing of the 29,000-ton battleship, Royal Oak, by a German submarine.*

OCTOBER 19. *Britain and France sign a fifteen-year mutual-assistance pact with Turkey. No mention is made of the Dardanelles and a protocol states that Turkey cannot be compelled to fight the Soviet Union.*

OCTOBER 24. *Foreign Minister von Ribbentrop of Germany tells Nazi party veterans at Danzig: "As far as Germany's relations with America are concerned, there is no possibility of any difference ever arising between the two countries."*

NOVEMBER 3. *Special session of United States Congress ends as House and Senate pass joint resolution repealing the arms embargo and forbidding American merchant shipping to enter the war zones.*

NOVEMBER 26. *Prime Minister Chamberlain delivers first radio broadcast since he announced war with Germany and repeats earlier statement that Allies are fighting for freedom and peace.*

NOVEMBER 28. *The Soviet government denounces nonagression pact with Finland.*

NOVEMBER 30. *Soviet troops invade Finland and Soviet airplanes shell Helsingfors and other cities.*

DECEMBER 17. *On orders from Berlin, the crew of the German pocket battleship, Graf Spee, scuttle their ship outside Montevideo.*

JANUARY 26, 1940. *Russian forces break strongest defenses of Mannerheim Line at Summa.*

FEBRUARY 16. *British destroyer Intrepid captures German steamer Altmark in Norwegian waters and frees 299 British seamen prisoners.*

MARCH 3. *Grand Admiral Raeder announces that Germany will wage uncompromising warfare on all British shipping.*

MARCH 7. *Russia and Finland agree to discuss an armistice.*

MARCH 12. *Russian and Finnish delegates sign a peace treaty which cedes sections of western Finland to Russia.*

MARCH 19. *Paul Reynaud forms a new French Cabinet with Daladier as Minister of Defense. On his first vote of confidence Reynaud receives a majority of one vote, the Socialists voting against him.*

MARCH 28. *Undersecretary of State Sumner Welles returns to Washington from a fact-finding survey of Europe and reports to the President.*

APRIL 7. *The Allies warn that they are mining the waters off the Norwegian coast. The governments of Norway and Holland protest this as violation of international law.*

WAR OF NERVES

[By September 15, at the end of two weeks of war, the Germans had virtually destroyed Poland. On September 17 the Russians occupied the eastern part of the country; and on September 28 a second German-Russian treaty accomplished the partition. Thereupon, for six and a half months, western Europe settled down into what certain grandstand managers in this country called a phony war.]

SEPTEMBER 29, 1939

I went to the country today for the first time in seven weeks. Whatever you may think of English politics, Englishmen's clothes or Englishwomen's hats, you would, I think, agree if you had been with me that the beauty of the English countryside has not been overadvertised. The light green of the fields outlined by the darker green hedges, city children playing in village streets, white clouds occasionally obscuring a brilliant autumn sun. But I went to the country not to enjoy its beauty but to look at one of the largest aviation training centers in Britain. I saw the art of camouflage raised to a new level of effectiveness, and I've seen camouflaged airports in half a dozen different countries in Europe.

Upon arrival, a sunburned youngster in an RAF uniform

suggested that he'd be willing to show us around. He was diffident and almost shy. This, I thought, is very nice. They have assigned someone from their press section to take us about. It wasn't until twenty minutes later that I realized we were being shown over the field and hangars by a young squadron leader, responsible for the most advanced phases of blind flying, different types of bombing and formation flying.

Since the outbreak of war the training period has been somewhat telescoped, but the officials seem to be confident of their ability to turn out fully qualified pilots in the shortest period. All of the men at this particular station had plenty of hours in the air before reporting for their advanced training. They apparently were not very much concerned about the progress of the war. Their job was to learn to fly, bomb, shoot, and navigate in the shortest possible time. Everything seemed clear cut and decisive. No confusion. After spending days and nights trying to understand the political side of this war the military side seemed very efficient and straightforward. The youth of those pilots gives one a very strange feeling. But as I was walking along today I heard a maintenance sergeant say, "There's one of those noisy Americans." That, I thought, was a little blunt but quite clear, though perhaps not in the British tradition of courtesy to foreigners.

I was somewhat relieved, upon talking with him, that he referred to one of the Harvard training ships that happened to be power diving at that moment. Those Harvards are American training ships purchased before the outbreak of the war and assembled over here, and they do make a noise that is quite individual.

Now coming back to London. Traveling on a train without lights of any kind, I felt as though we were passing through an endless tunnel. In my compartment there were two Air Force pilots. We sat there in the dark and talked— not about the war or flying or yet the American Neutrality Act. Nothing was said about the burden of the war budget. I happened to know the part of England from which they came, and we talked about that; about the single clump of trees that stands on the top of the hill like an Indian-feather headdress, about the local pub, and the vicar who seems to be having trouble navigating his bicycle along the winding country lanes these dark nights.

Now to come back to London. The general feeling seems to be that the Russian-German agreement is an attempt to frighten Great Britain and France. No one minimizes the gravity of the situation, but I haven't seen any evidences of fright. Tonight's broadcasts indicate that any peace proposals based upon present conditions will probably be rejected in advance, both here and in Paris. One news agency declares that the Soviet Ambassador in London, Mr. Maisky, told Lord Halifax the day before yesterday that the Soviet Union was prepared to accept a trade agreement with Britain and that the Soviet government intended to maintain its policy of neutrality. But that was day before yesterday.

OCTOBER 2, 1939

This war is still in a stage where speeches are important. The question, "Well, what did you think of Churchill's speech?" has been put to me by many of my English friends last night and this morning. They want to know what

America thought of it, whether or not it is likely to have any influence on the neutrality debate and whether or not the First Sea Lord was well advised in talking of the American Civil War, or rather, the War Between the States, when he said, "All the heroism of the South could not redeem their cause from the stain of slavery, just as all the courage and skill which the Germans always show in war will not free them from the reproach of Nazism, its intolerance and brutality."

Well, those are questions I can't answer. I'm not even inclined to write my Congressman about it all. My job is to tell you not what America thought of his speech but what Britain thought of it, and that is a fairly easy task. Most of my friends seem to think it was the best broadcast made by any Cabinet minister since the outbreak of the war. They liked it. It has increased Mr. Churchill's reputation as a leader. He, more than anyone else in this government, has been right in his predictions of European governments during the last several years. Whether or not he was right in his comments concerning Russia remains, as Mr. Churchill himself said, to be seen. He said nothing calculated to hasten the active participation of Russia in this war. It is significant that he made no reference directly or by implication to any possibility of a patched-up peace.

I think the *Daily Telegraph* reflects the reaction of most Londoners when, in commenting on Mr. Churchill's speech, it says: "This was the voice of Britain speaking."

Now, as I remember, political speeches in the United States generally have some reaction on the stock market, and you might care to know that after Mr. Churchill's speech last night the stock market here in London opened

quiet but steady this morning. London today still looks to
Moscow and the results of the Turkish-Soviet conversations.
Those talks, according to the latest advices here, may last
for several days. London looks, too, to the western front for
a possible German offensive, once the peace drive fails, if
it does. I have not yet found any responsible official here
who believes that that peace drive will succeed.

OCTOBER 15, 1939

This afternoon I spent two hours and a gallon of precious
gasoline looking at London from Hampstead Heath to St.
Paul's. It was a cold, wet Sunday afternoon with not many
people on the streets, few cruising taxicabs. They don't
cruise any more. They just sit still, waiting for passengers,
in order to conserve gasoline. Practically no private cars
were about. Green canvas deck chairs, empty and wet, were
scattered through the park. Piles of sand waiting to be shuf-
fled into packs. A few new signs in Harley Street, the home
of London's medical aristocracy. Signs reading, HOUSE TO
LET or LEASE TO BE DISPOSED OF. Those expensive shops in
Bond Street, all of them sandbagged; the windows boarded
up; others crisscrossed with strips of brown paper to prevent
shattering. Tailor-shop windows full of uniforms. They used
to display well-cut dinner clothes and tweed sport jackets.
Windows of the women's shops filled with heavy-wool evening dresses and sturdy shoes. Some of those shops show a
new kind of women's wear—a sort of coverall arrangement
with zippers and a hood—one piece affairs, easy to put on.
They are to be worn when the sirens sound. So they are
called appropriately enough siren suits. There are big black

and red arrows pointing the way to air-raid shelters. A discreet little sign in the window of the most expensive automobile showrooms in London, saying BUSINESS AS USUAL.

Up in Great Fulton Street there are many automobile showrooms that have simply folded up. The owners have gone away. Then down the Mall, with the first autumn leaves plastered on wet pavements; into Whitehall past deserted Downing Street. The Cenotaph, with a few new wreaths under the dripping Union Jacks. Then along the Embankment. Barges loaded with waste paper, riding at anchor in the muddy Thames. White bands of paint on the trees, on the curbstones, letter boxes, and lampposts. White lines dividing the roadway. I wonder if anyone knows how many gallons of white paint have been used in London.

Fleet Street, the home of London's newspapers. Bigger and better sandbags and more of them. Then determined-looking pigeons eating crumbs in the courtyard in front of St. Paul's. Then back down Ludgate Hill. Fleet Street again, down the Strand to Trafalgar Square. More pigeons. Lots of special policemen but few pedestrians. Incidentally, the policemen are not as impressive as they used to be. Bobbies wearing tin hats instead of their famous helmets and their khaki haversacks contrasting with their blue uniforms. I watched them and felt that it had somehow all lost the dignified solemnity of peacetime. The steamship offices are still around Trafalgar Square but they no longer advertise their sailing date. Admiral Nelson continues to look down from the top of his tall column. He seems almost out of place without a tin helmet and a gas mask. The Athenaeum, one of the most famous clubs in London, from which old gentlemen write letters to the London *Times*, has a fresh coat of white paint. Eros, the graceful statue of the god of love, no longer aims an arrow at the traffic that swirls around Piccadilly Circus, because Eros has been removed to safety for the duration of the war. The streets are clean and orderly. The sandbags seem to have softened the contour of some of London's harsh-looking buildings. Occasionally, if you glance into a mews, that's a blind alley to us, you see an ambulance or taxicab with a fire pump attached, sitting there ready for action.

In many ways London on a wet Sunday afternoon in wartime resembles London on a wet Sunday afternoon in peacetime. Londoners like to spend such afternoons at home, and I don't blame them. The real change comes at night to London. Then it is a city of sound, generally slow, cautious sounds—what it really looks like at night I can't tell you because I've never been able to see more of it than has been disclosed by the beam of my puny flashlight.

Now for a quick summary of the past week. The convoy of merchant ships by naval escort and airplanes seems to be functioning efficiently. The week has given the British forces in France an opportunity to consolidate their positions and perfect their system of supply. The diplomatic developments have, in the British view, been all to Germany's disadvantage. It is pointed out that M. Daladier gave the first answer to Herr Hitler's peace proposals, thus demonstrating that the German efforts to divide Britain and France have failed.

The Russian moves in the Baltic, whatever the methods used to achieve them, are also considered damaging to the German cause. The change in the Balkans, where many things have been determined by fear of Germany, and where

Moscow now seems to be calling the tune, has not been a disappointment to the British either. And finally the progress of the neutrality bill in the American Senate has developed pretty much along a stiff and hopeful line. On the other side of the ledger must be placed the continued difficulty encountered in reaching a satisfactory solution of the problems raised by the Indian National Congress. There is still criticism on the economic front. There is still a demand for the creation of an Economic General Staff and an effective and all-powerful Ministry of Supply. The appointment of Lord Stamp as adviser on economic co-ordination, a job to which he is apparently to devote only part of his time, is not believed to have solved the problem entirely. There are still many questions to be solved in the field of education. In many areas, such as London and Manchester, there are no schools at all and some of the evacuation areas have schools working in double shifts. Many students who formerly attended technical schools now find themselves in areas where no such schools are available.

There is a certain amount of discussion concerning the future leadership of the Labour party. It is possible that Mr. Herbert Morrison, generally considered to be the ablest administrator of the party, who is now Chairman of the London County Council—that is a job similar to that held by Mayor LaGuardia in New York—may emerge as a dominant figure in His Majesty's opposition. Bill Henry reports that it has been a quiet day for the Royal Air Force in France. The weather has been bad and there has been little flying. Many men went to church. Others stood about and discussed the war. Mr. Henry said they talked about it just like diplomats.

OCTOBER 21, 1939

The British press this morning is busily engaged in denouncing the newest effort of the Nazi propaganda ministry. This seems to be a German answer to the pamphlet raids of the British on Germany. The Germans are utilizing the British and Danish post offices to carry on this work instead of airplanes. Letters are being mailed from Denmark to responsible business firms in England. The unmarked envelopes contain large sheets of paper—headed *British Poison Gas for Poland*—and allege that a Swiss doctor when asked to examine wounded German soldiers in Poland reported that they suffered from the effects of mustard-gas poisoning. The British War Office has twice denied the accusation that Britain furnished the Poles with poison gas and this morning the *Daily Express* claims to have interviewed that same Swiss doctor in Geneva. The British interview states that the doctor said his diagnosis—that the German soldiers suffered from the effects of mustard gas—was correct, but when he asked when the gas poisoning had taken place he was taken to a shell hole near a bridge. Here, the doctor maintains in the British interview, "he merely could smell the fumes of lime chlorate," which is an antidote for mustard gas, and that's all he saw. The conclusion reached by the British is that Germans are stacking the cards with poison-gas reports in order to utilize this deadly weapon themselves on the western front.

Another German propaganda effort is being discussed this morning. That's a report that Hitler will make a separate peace offer to France, hoping to weaken her will to victory by attractive offers. Then, after splitting the Allies, Hitler would wage a war to the finish with Britain. This report is characterized here as a desperate move by a desperate man. The possibility of a wedge being driven between the Allies is laughed at scornfully in England. Meantime it is reported that the second 100,000 members of the British Expeditionary Force are moving up to the front line in France and this morning the second group of 250,000 men to be drafted are registering all over England. This is the so-called "twenty-one" class, men between the ages of twenty and twenty-two. It is expected that at least a month will pass before they will be actually called up for training. Many of these young men are unemployed and while wages are going up they are not going up as fast as the cost of living. The textile workers have received a 12½% wage increase, so have the railroad men. They were on the verge of striking for more money at the start of the war. The railroaders have received about a quarter of what they asked for.

Londoners are not reading much news about this war because there isn't much news, so they have turned to reading books about the last war. The circulation figures of lending libraries have gone up. The troops in France will be doing some reading, too. Some indication of what they will read is to be found in a catalogue of 1321 titles officially recommended for sending to the troops at the front. There is a lot of religion, fiction, travel, exploration, and adventure. The best seller, written by the man the troops are pledged to destroy—*Mein Kampf*, by Adolf Hitler—is on the list. So is *Capital* by Karl Marx; so is *Under Fire*, by Barbusse, the pacifist. And also on the list is Tolstoy's *War and Peace*.

While the diplomats are busy and the soldiers wait, Britain's inventors are active. One man advocates a new style in glasses, the lens and blinders are to be made of cardboard. Naturally that prevents you seeing anything at all, but this particular gentleman insists that if they are worn consistently day and night you won't notice the blackout. There is another report of a highly practical invention. I can't vouch for this—I just read about it in a newspaper. It's an attachment to be fitted to lampposts. When a pedestrian approaches within a given distance of a lamppost on a dark night, that lamppost emits a loud squeak or shout. I suspect that most of the inventive genius of Britain is being devoted to scientific researches of a more serious nature.

OCTOBER 22, 1939

Twice today air-raid sirens sounded in Britain. No bombs were dropped.

Here in London Parliament continues to resemble a council of state. Plenty of questions are asked and at times debated heatedly, particularly when the home front is under discussion. The Labour party harasses the government's front benches with questions about allowances for soldiers' wives, profiteering, Indian policy, and the qualifications of men appointed to handle a new department. There is a considerable number of opposition members who maintain that Mr. Chamberlain is fighting a war on two fronts—against Hitlerism and against changes in the social and economic structure of Britain. They profess to see a reflection of this policy in his ministerial appointments. They claim that too much of the supply and transport of Britain has been handed over to big business. There is no indication that open party warfare will be resumed. Party discipline while not at peacetime strength is still strong. Many members are concerned about British propaganda in neutral capitals. Reports from such countries as Holland and Belgium, as well as certain Scandinavian countries, indicate that the Germans are more active, spending more money, maintaining larger staffs. One hears so many stories that the British representatives are hard-pressed to counter the propaganda efforts of Dr. Goebbels' representatives. Naturally there is much interest in what is happening in America.

Machinery has been set up to study the trend and tone of American broadcasting and newspapers. One is frequently asked what the reaction of America was to lectures given by various Britishers who are now visiting you. Any American news broadcaster can be sure of a regular audience of at least three people in Europe these days. Men in Britain, France, and Germany are taking down his words.

I can't talk about the weather over here tonight. But I can tell you that there have been unprecedented floods in the midlands which have disturbed a number of people. There are also reports of floods in the Siegfried Line. But naturally that's not so disturbing to Britishers. The weather on the western front has apparently been as bad as it could be. And the combination of weather and German diplomacy aimed at dividing Britain and France was given as the excuse for the practical cessation of hostilities. But somehow one doesn't feel like complaining about the rain and wind. Autumn has arrived and we expect British weather. But, for a few days at least, we saw England at its best. Bright sun; furried white clouds; brown fields contrasting with green pasture land. Pale-gray ground fogs twisting and smoking knee-deep between the trees and along the stream.

Dead wet leaves striking down into the fog. One may be allowed to hope that the survivors of this war may still be able to see and feel the beauty of the English countryside; able to enjoy those winding trails through the Black Forest and the glory of the Necker Valley where it meets the Rhine.

But that's the sort of thing that doesn't crop up in the course of man-made conversation nowadays. Something is happening to conversation in London. There isn't much of it. You meet a friend, exchange guesses about the latest diplomatic move, inquire about a mutual friend who has been called up, and then fall silent. Nothing seems important, not even the weather. The experts, the political experts, not the weather experts, sound as though they were trying to convince themselves of their own expertness. Don't get the idea that these people are discouraged or defeated. They are confident of winning this war, somehow or other. They still exercise the Briton's right to complain. They haven't lost their sense of humor. But it seems that in this war, courage and patience are the supreme virtues. Wit, happiness, manners, and conversation sink gradually. Conversation is about to become a casualty.

NOVEMBER 18, 1939

Here's news about 500,000 natives of Britain who remain completely unperturbed, although two enormous, unexploded bombs lay in their midst for almost a week. The experience might have struck fear into the hearts of the bravest of these natives. But, like their kind throughout the world, they know no fear. You see, these natives are native oysters. Last week, a Royal Air Force reconnaissance plane made a forced landing in a heavy fog on an oyster bed exposed by the tide. In order to take off again, the plane was forced to leave its heavy bombs behind. Surrounding them were some half million of Britain's choicest and most expensive oysters. The local oystermen were naturally perturbed. They thought that driftwood or the action of the tide might explode the bombs and destroy their oyster crops. If this occurred, they said the concussion might endanger the supply of entire generations of oysters yet unborn. The Royal Air Force assured the oystermen that their fears were ungrounded. The bombs would not explode and ruin the oysters. Nevertheless, they removed them as soon as possible. Now all is well. And a half-million oysters can open their shells without danger of total destruction.

NOVEMBER 26, 1939

Here are a few things that struck me as interesting in Mr. Chamberlain's broadcast tonight, his first since war was declared. He began by saying losses had been and would be announced promptly. That was in answer to the many who have complained of the lack of news and the fact that other nations have had in some cases more news of Britain's war than have British subjects. His own health and strength, he said, were unimpaired. That was in answer to a few stories claiming that his advanced age and the strain of handling the War Cabinet were proving too much and he might have to retire. The Prime Minister said the Allies would choose the time and place to strike. Meanwhile, the blockade was doing its work. That was his answer to those who say, "Let's get on with the war."

Britain's war aim is the defeat of Germany and the military aggressiveness for which that nation stands, said Mr. Chamberlain. If it could be achieved without bloodshed, so much the better. That statement will, I expect, be used in the radio, leaflet, and underground campaign being conducted by Britain against the present German government.

So far as peace aims are concerned, the Prime Minister wants a new Europe with a new spirit. He hopes for a constant flow of trade which will lift the standard of living of Europe. Armaments will, he hopes, be gradually reduced, and the final settlement will require machinery the nature of which cannot now be determined. But he held out the hope to Germany that a German government which presumably would have to meet the Allies' requirements would be able to sit about the table and help in creating a new order.

There has been time to talk with only a few political observers since Mr. Chamberlain's broadcast, but the general opinion seems to be that his stock will go up as a result of it.

I have been doing a little research this week, looking into the general subject of London night life. Business is good; has, in fact, improved since war came. There are more dance bands playing in London's West End now than in the months before peace went underground. Many establishments where one could eat without musical distraction in the old days have now engaged small orchestras. Customers want to dance. Places like the Embassy Club, Qualinos, the

Paradise, Café de Paris, and that padded room called the Four Hundred are jammed nearly every night. People come early and stay late. I left one place at 3:30 the other morning. No one else showed any disposition to leave and so far as I know they may be there still, singing *The Beer Barrel Polka* and trying to dance on an overcrowded floor. Uniforms and civilian clothes are about evenly divided, but practically no one wears formal evening dress. That's a change from prewar days. Officers are inclined to remove their Sam Browne belts when dancing, although that practice is frowned upon by the War Office.

There are plenty of women in uniform, too. It's a little hard to tell their rank and unit in the half-light that seems to be an indispensable part of night-club equipment. A sergeant of the Women's Auxiliary Fire Service being pushed about the dance floor by a private, wearing the battle uniform of the regular Army, with heavy service loops, may barge into a wing commander of the Air Force and his smartly dressed companion. Turning about to apologize they may come face to face with a man in tweed jacket and flannel trousers, dancing with a girl in a gingham dress. All this in a place where a few months ago evening dress was as important as the ability to pay the check.

Prices have gone up, but that doesn't seem to matter. The entertainers are having a grand time. Their audiences aren't as critical as they used to be. They've come to dance and be amused, prepared to laugh and applaud no matter what's provided in the way of entertainment. Occasionally you'll see a quiet, sober-faced couple sitting in a remote corner engaged in serious conversation. But not often. Maybe they're talking about what they'll do when all this has passed away, or they may be deciding whether or not they can afford another drink. I don't know what people talk about in such surroundings.

There is something of a speakeasy atmosphere about London's night clubs. It seems that those who frequent restaurants and clubs are either more fatalistic or more careless than the average Londoner; anyway, few of them carry gas masks. The managers still seem frightened of admitting fresh air, and a friend of mine maintains that the only time he's really had a desire to put on his gas mask was in a crowded night club at four in the morning. But don't get the idea that all London sits about waiting for darkness, dancing, and drink. Plenty of people here know nothing and care less about London's night clubs and the night-club life. Radio is a constant source of information and entertainment. There are letters to be written to friends and relatives, and some people seem to have found that the extra hours of sleep help to pass away the long hours of the blackout. I expect they're right.

NOVEMBER 27, 1939

At 3:30 on the afternoon of Thursday, November 23, the British armed merchant cruiser, *Rawalpindi*, was cruising off Iceland as part of the northern patrol. Her captain sighted an enemy ship. Smoke floats were lit and thrown into the water to enable the *Rawalpindi* to escape. A second enemy ship was seen coming up to starboard. A shot bounced across the bows of the *Rawalpindi* but she continued on her course. Captain Kalady of the British ship had a look through his glasses and said, "It's the *Deutschland*, all right," and ordered his crew to action stations. Course was altered to bring the enemy on the starboard quarter, then the *Deutschland* opened with the first salvo of her eleven-inch guns. The range was 10,000 yards—nearly six miles. The *Rawalpindi* replied with her four starboard six-inch guns. The *Deutschland*'s third salvo extinguished the lights and smashed the electric winches of her ammunition carriers. The fourth salvo carried away the bridge and wire-less room of the *Rawalpindi*. By this time the second German ship was hammering the British merchant cruiser from the port side. The fight lasted about half an hour. By that time every gun on the *Rawalpindi* was out of action and the ship was ablaze between the fo'c'sle and the boom. The British ship continued to burn until eight o'clock when she turned turtle and foundered with all hands who had not escaped in the two undamaged lifeboats. A British cruiser then arrived and the two German ships made off in the darkness. That's the story of the first naval action of this war as released by the British Admiralty.

The King today signed the order for the seizure of German exports. The complete text will be published tomorrow. It will be accompanied by an explanatory note which will set forth the British claim that close attention has been paid to the interests of neutrals. The order will not come into force for a few days. Meanwhile, the Japanese have pointed out that Britain promised on September 22 that no action would be taken even in British territorial waters against neutral vessels carrying goods which had been produced or manufactured in Germany. It is claimed here that not a single British ship has been put out of action by German bombing planes since the war began and it is believed that warships have demonstrated their ability to defend themselves against enemy aircraft.

The General Secretary of the Civil Service Clerical Association talked about revolution today. "Some wars," he said, "end in revolution. This one is beginning with one." He said that a silent revolution is taking place in Britain. A revolution in the distribution of income. This important association leader pointed out that while the wages of certain of the working classes will rise as the cost of living goes up, there is another part of the working class which is suffering. These are the unemployed, the pensioners, and those whose salaries are fixed. Their income is fixed and their salaries do not increase as the cost of living goes up. If the cost of living continues to rise, the standard of living of these classes will sink in relation to the workers with sliding incomes. The General Secretary of the Civil Service Association said the government will immediately tackle the problem of these sudden changes and the constant rise in living costs.

The other afternoon I spent several hours underground, studying the central control station of London's air-raid-precaution system. One man can sit in that room and move ambulances, stretcher parties, gas-decontamination squads, and repair parties, just as though he had them on the end of a string. The maps covering the walls resemble those in an army headquarters. The whole system is linked to local units by direct telephone and if the telephones don't work there are motorcycle dispatch riders standing by to carry messages. If London is bombed, one could sit in that room and by reading colored pins and discs on the maps tell just where bridges have been blown up, where fire engines are needed, where additional ambulances are required, and the position of reserve units which might be needed. It was quiet down there the other day. The elaborate maps on which one could follow the approach of enemy aircraft were clear. The bright little pins which means gas or railroads destroyed or serious fire were sitting in a little box like toy soldiers. The telephone operators, young girls who might have been college sophomores at home, sat at their instruments, knitting or reading. One was reading the life of *Mme Curie*, another Tolstoy's *War and Peace*, and the latest detective thrillers were also in evidence. Occasionally they practice a little—the telephone rings, the operator takes down a message, passes it through a slot to the control officer, and in a few minutes' time an ambulance brigade or a couple of fire engines go racing through the streets in the remote part of London on a practice trip. The whole scheme seemed to be efficient and at the same time easy to operate. The appeal of the British Admiralty for sailors to man the mine sweepers was answered by long lines of merchant sailors and fishermen signing on at Grimsby yesterday and today. The Admiralty also asked for a small fishing ship to join the mine-sweeping fleet. This was met with an immediate offer of some two hundred drifters and trawlers, all working fishing craft.

The Minister of Food will announce in the House of Commons tomorrow the date for the introduction of rationing in Britain and it is reported from Oslo that the Norwegian Nobel Committee has reached a decision on its annual peace award. It has decided not to award a peace prize for 1939.

NOVEMBER 29, 1939

The second day of the new session of Parliament produced some interesting comment. Labour members warned that the country may be facing an industrial unrest as the result of rising prices, low wages, and inadequate old-age pensions and soldiers' allowances. Sir John Simon, who controls the treasury out of which twenty-four million dollars a day is pouring for the support of the war, spoke of the fearful sacrifices that may be demanded of the British people before this war is finished. The rich he said had been pretty severely soaked already and there wasn't enough of them to produce any considerable fraction of the total amount of money required. He went on to say that unemployment allowances will be increased before Christmas in view of the rising cost of living.

If you were an Englishman with an income of say $50 a week, out of which you can save $10 a week, I think you would be baffled as to what to do with that $10. Whether to save it or spend it. One Cabinet minister has asked you to avoid unnecessary spending in order that you may loan your savings to the government. Another has urged you to spend in order to keep trade going. Advertisements urge you to buy now because prices will be going up. Economists tell you that prices will go up higher and faster than wages. No one has drawn the line where patriotic spending should end and patriotic saving should begin. Mr. Keynes, one of Britain's economists, says that people really haven't got any choice—that they must have either compulsory saving or compulsory inflation. It just happens. It spreads an illusion of prosperity. But basically it reduces the purchasing power of the working classes and the unemployed as well as those with a fixed income. Mr. Keynes concludes that, in general, the British public is not in favor of any plan and that this indifference accounts for the fact that national production has increased very little during the three months of the war.

Well, while you are wondering what to do with those ten dollars you have saved each week, over and above your basic living costs, you see government posters in the street which tell you to LEND TO DEFEND THE RIGHT TO BE FREE. That's the problem that faces you—should you save or spend. However, if you're like many Britishers, you can't save that ten dollars; if you could save it in peacetime, your unemployed relatives, the cost of supporting your evacuated children in other homes, and the rising cost of necessities and luxuries just eat it all up.

DECEMBER 1, 1939

A few hours after I finished talking with you last night, I left London for a British seaport. I can't tell you its name, but early this morning I saw a harborful of small ships— tough-looking, rusty little ships, they were—trawlers that had been scarred and hammered by north-Atlantic gales. Black smoke was pouring from their funnels. Many of them old; some still with fish scales in their holds. I saw some of them arriving from Grimsby, Hull, Aberdeen, Fleetwood, and the other fishing ports of Britain. They were coming in answer to the Navy's call for more trawlers to meet the German mine menace. Many of them still flew that familiar red duster—the flag of the British merchant navy. They had not yet been commissioned. Some of them had already been transformed into mine sweepers. They carried a small gun on top of a toadstool-like steel structure forward. Depth charges, looking like squat milk cans, were chained up now, ready to be dropped overboard by the flick of a lever. The men in those ships are small. They are of all ages and voices. Some of them come from the rocky coast of Scotland and others from the quiet, dark waters on the coast of Essex. Often they have trouble understanding one another. They wear no uniform, but their ships, after they have been commissioned, fly the white ensign of the British Navy. I saw weather-beaten skippers talk to the port captain with hands in pockets and pipe in mouth. All of them were fishermen in peacetime and their job now is to fish for mines. Those ships are no place for men with faulty digestion. One cook told me quite frankly that he was accustomed to serving Irish stew for breakfast and that other than that he just made tea and did light cooking.

The normal ship's complement is sixteen men. I went aboard one of those trawlers and they nosed her out beyond the breakwater. There was a stiff breeze blowing and those ships are not dry. When we were well clear of the harbor, something that looked like a medium-sized door was flung out from the gallows, or steel bow, through which so many trawling lines have run in peacetime. Attached to it is a light steel float with red flag on top of it. It looks very much like an oversize tuna fish that has been speared by a red flag. A three-by-four-inch cable was paid out from a steel winch and the float drifted astern and to port. That steel cable, called the sweepline, is rough in order that it will saw through the anchor line of a mine. After about five hundred yards of sweepline had been paid out, the heavy piece of steel, which looked like an overgrown window shutter and was attached to the line, was dropped into the water and it immediately forced the sweepline about thirty feet below the surface. Thus we have five hundred yards of steel cable cutting through the water on our port side about thirty feet below the surface, feeling for mines. The float with its little red flag bounces along the way to port and just a little astern. The sweepline throbbed and hummed in the blocks as we move out to sea and swing down the commercial shipping lanes. We stand and watch the float because if the sweep wire does not saw the mine anchor in two it slides along until it hits a big knifelike affair just beneath the float and then the mine bobs to the surface and after that it's exploded by shellfire. I was told that we had a reasonable chance of picking up a mine, but nothing happened.

It was rough and wet out there today and I wasn't particularly sorry when we saw the white cliffs of England, looking like a dirty-white sheet hanging from the edge of a green roof, just before dusk. I crawled behind the forward gun support with two seamen. The wind had freshened and our little trawler was taking plenty of water aboard. Brown, cold water it was, too. For me the day was interesting and represented a new adventure, but those fishermen sailors do it every day and many nights. All for about sixty cents a day, plus family allowance. Heroes aren't expensive in Britain's most famous mine-sweeping patrol, but it takes plenty of four-o'clock-in-the-morning courage to do that job.

I spent most of my time today talking with deck hands. They did their job in a quiet, matter-of-fact way, just as though they were fishing for herring rather than mines.

There was no blowing of whistles, saluting, no shouting of orders. When the sweep was finally brought in, we all had a cup of the strongest tea I have ever tasted. The Scottish skipper said he hoped to tie his boat up somewhere north of the border again. The deck hand looked forward to taking care of the cabbage patch he has somewhere in England. Another was jubilant because he just won the lottery permitting him to have Christmas day ashore. I wonder how many men on both sides of this war, both on the sea and beneath it, would rather be doing something else. When the motor boat put me ashore I stood on the dock and watched the stern of that rusty, weather-beaten, twenty-year-old trawler lift and twist as her bow met the water. She was going out again, wallowing up the channel, heading, I suspect, for more dangerous waters than those swept today. That's a quick look at Britain's mine-sweeping patrol. New mines will require new treatment. A lot of schemes are now being studied and tried out. I wish I had time to tell you more of the last twenty hours' impressions. Mine-sweeping may not be magnificent—it's not even high dramatics—but it's war.

DECEMBER 11, 1939

There is a current of change in tone and content of the more serious weekly publications in Britain. For weeks the main subject for discussion and debate was war aims. Many plans were evolved. Editors received many letters setting forth different schemes for the organization of a postwar Europe—but there has been a change. The talk now is of financial affairs. How is the war to be paid for? How can eco-

nomic warfare be carried on without driving down the
standard of living of the workers? Where is the money for
arms, armies, navies, and civil defense coming from? Who
should pay and how much? Should the individuals save or
spend? There is no agreement—just as there was no agreement about war aims—but it is interesting to note that the
discussion has moved to the realm of finance—the mode,
the money. There was a consideration of the postwar recon-
struction and study of methods to be employed in financing
the peace question of Europe. The absence of large-scale
fighting makes it possible to follow more easily the social,
political, and economic development brought about by the
war, but it doesn't seem to be easy for men to reach the
same conclusions as to what is happening.

Sometimes, while reading long articles, listening to
speeches, asking questions of so-called experts, one gets the
strange feeling that perhaps no one really understands at
all—that the machine is out of control, that we are all passengers on an express train traveling at high speed through
a dark tunnel toward an unknown destiny. We sit and talk
as convincingly as we can, speaking words someone else has
used. The suspicion recurs that the train may have no engineer, no one who can handle it—no one who can bring us
to a standstill. Maybe that's why more people seem to be
reading their Bibles these days. Perhaps that's why this war
has not produced a poet or a really popular song, why it
hasn't even produced much hatred.

Here's an interesting but unimportant wartime phenome-
non in Britain. All technical and documentary evidence
about the so-called English climate has been suppressed.
We aren't told what the weather is going to be, what it is,

nor yet what it has been. Broadcasts don't mention the weather, nor do the papers. It must be two weeks old before it's considered a fit subject for public comment. Englishmen love to talk about their weather. Continentals have claimed that the Englishman's real home is in his barometer, that he is unable to forget it even during romantic moonlit intervals. In prewar days Britain seemed to be a small island located halfway between a deep depression over Iceland and a high-pressure ridge near the Azores. Any Englishman could talk about his weather for fifteen minutes without repeating himself. But all that is changed. The weather is now dismissed with a few curt but not always courteous phrases. The weather prophets prepare their prognostications for the fighting forces, and the layman takes what comes. If it should rain soup, the poor man would have no spoon, because he would have had no warning.

I shall now talk about the weather. Two weeks ago I stood at my office window and watched London's pedestrians hurrying along the streets below. Two women out of three carried gas masks; they all carried umbrellas. Every other man carried a gas mask slung over his shoulder, but two out of three carried umbrellas. Your reporter concluded that on that particular day Londoners considered the weather more menacing than German gas bombs that might rain from the sky. It is even reported that a general has been seen on duty with a cold. When I was in the army it seemed inconceivable that a general should have a cold.

DECEMBER 14, 1939

I thought maybe you'd like to hear something about the

young men who don't want to fight, the conscientious objectors, those who refuse to fight for King and country. Roughly three out of every hundred men between the ages of twenty and twenty-two ask to be exempt from military service. If you are interested only in armies and not the individuals, then this story is not for you. But if the three in every hundred interest you, the misfits, cowards, men of moral courage—call them what you will—then here is their story, or at least part of it.

The council chambers of Fuller Town Hall look like a courtroom. Five elderly men sit behind a bench: a judge, the president of a university, the senior civil servant, the secretary of a trade union, and a city alderman. They all wear plain clothes and appear to be eminently respectable gentlemen. The little gallery at the back of the room is crowded with a variety of persons. Most of them are leaning forward. The atmosphere is just between that of a church and a courtroom. Down on the floor all alone looking up at the five men is a boy. He is twenty years and seven months old. He is small and wiry, with sandy hair, an Irishman if there ever was one. He has been drafted and has asked for exemption as a conscientious objector. The five men on the bench must decide what to do with him. They question him. Why doesn't he want to fight? Because to him it would be murder. War settles nothing. Four of his cousins were killed fighting in the Irish troubles and nothing was settled. The questions and answers are informal. The boy is given plenty of time to formulate his answers. Would his conscience permit him to continue in a factory? It would. There is a whispered conversation on the bench, and the judge tells him that he will be registered as a conscientious

objector and need not go to war. And up in the gallery an
elderly lady leans back in her chair and relaxes.

Next comes a fat, dark-haired boy. He works in a shell
factory and is prepared to go on working there but he
doesn't want to fight. He doesn't like war. Another conference on the bench. The young munitions worker is not a
true conscientious objector and he must go to the army.

Next comes a boy with long hair and a thin face. For two
years he has been a full-time worker in a religious order,
preaching and distributing pamphlets. He refuses to don a
uniform and take an oath because he says he recognizes
only the authority of God. The university president asks his
interpretation of Christ's attitude toward war. The boy re-
plies in a steady voice, using many quotations from the
Bible. The judge asks the objector if the latter feels no responsibility to the state. "Certainly," says the boy, "but I
refuse to kill or accept the authority of anyone but God."
The discussion is fascinating—this youngster against the five
men who are trying to determine what is in his mind and
trying to test the validity of his conscience. After nearly a
half-hour, he is asked if he would work on a farm as a
civilian. This he agrees to do; agrees, that is, provided that
he can continue to preach.

An Oxford student is next. He says that he is willing to
defend Britain, but he doesn't believe that this is a defensive war. Rather than wreck the world he would submit to
German domination. He quotes Chamberlain as saying that
the war is being fought in defense of small nations and goes
on to say that he is not interested in the small nations and is
prepared to go to jail rather than fight. His case takes twenty
minutes before it is decided he needn't fight.

Then there is a young Welshman, who belongs to the Welsh Nationalist party that wants independence for Wales. He tells his judges he is sorry he is a British subject and refuses to recognize the right of England (which he considers a foreign country) to send him out to fight. If Wales were attacked, he goes on, he would defend it, but he argues that the Welsh should have the right to decide what they shall fight for and what they shall not fight for. The men on the bench tried to reason with him, pointing out that Welsh members of Parliament voted for war, but he will have none of it. He refuses to recognize that a majority must be right. Decision has been reserved in his case and, when the issue is settled, an important precedent will be established. And on it goes. I've seen twenty of those boys pass before the conscientious objectors' tribunal: a man who refuses to take an oath to anyone except to his God; men who say that they refuse to recognize the right of Britain to send them off to war because they are Welshmen. Every case I saw received careful attention and plenty of time. The men on the bench seemed really to try to understand what the boys were talking about. I talked with those men on the bench for over an hour and I asked them for a definition of conscience and they couldn't give me one. But they all agreed that a British subject should have the right to say what his conscience dictates before he is forced to fight.

They are handing out a sort of rough justice where fixed legal principles cannot apply. They try to test a man's sincerity and the depth of his convictions. If the man is just afraid of getting killed, they can't let him off because apparently that doesn't involve conscience. If the applicant feels that fighting would be a crime, in a moral sense, he is likely to be sent to work on a farm or in the woods or in some other form of noncombatant work. Or perhaps sent to the ambulance corps or first-aid station; although I saw one medical student getting complete exemption because he was convinced he would be committing a sin if he patched up men in order that they might go back to kill other men.

Some of those boys may have been faking. Maybe they were cowards. I don't know. But I saw at least a few of them leave the courtroom, clutching the only thing many of us have left, that indefinable thing called conscience.

DECEMBER 23, 1939

London's editorial writers had a difficult assignment this morning. They had to write about Christmas. They write at length but with a degree of uncertainty. They all agree that it's a strange Christmas. Many people in this country remember other wartime Christmases, but this one will be different because evacuation has divided families as never before. It is admitted that the message of good will among men cannot be extended to the enemy, but those who fight with Britain receive good will in full measure. Two comments about Christmas are worth quoting, I think. The first is from the *Daily Telegraph*: "The clock ticks out the little lives of men, but neither war nor time itself can tick out those deepest instincts of the human heart for which childhood is both the keeper and the interpreter. Christmas-tide and all that it signifies will survive even all that saddens and subdues it in the present year of grace." The other comment comes from a regular sidewalk artist who draws pictures on the pavement outside our office. His greeting is:

"Best Wishes for another Christmas." He says his greeting seems to be very popular.

David Low, Britain's number-one cartoonist, presents a sketch in this afternoon's *Evening Standard* showing Santa Claus complete with reindeer and sleigh flying through the air with shells bursting all around. He captions this drawing: AN UNIDENTIFIED AIRCRAFT APPEARED OVER THE EAST COAST LAST NIGHT. OUR GUNS OPENED FIRE AND THE STRANGER AFTER DROPPING SOME SUSPICIOUS-LOOKING BUNDLES MADE OFF WILDLY IN ALL DIRECTIONS. Mr. Low also gives us a picture of Neville Chamberlain driving a heavily laden stage coach on a snowy road to an urgent appointment with destiny. A trunk on the roof of the stage coach is marked SACRED RIGHTS OF PROPERTY. Mr. Low's famous figure, Colonel Blimp, is a passenger and he asserts, "We beat this fellow Napoleon before and we'll do it again."

The matter of Allied assistance to Finland still engages the attention of most diplomatic experts. Some of them claim that Russian equipment is so old and inferior as to make unnecessary the sending to Finland of up-to-date guns, airplanes, and other equipment. In other words, obsolete British and French guns and planes may be found adequate if employed against the older Russian material.

Some people expect that Signor Mussolini, perhaps with the assistance of the Vatican, will fly another peace kite during the Christmas holidays. There's been a rumor, but only a rumor, in London for the past several days that a large-scale loan for Italy is in the making. One well-known bridge-playing diplomat was asked the other day what he thought of the progress of the war. His reply was, "We have not yet cut for partners." There is division of opinion as to which partnership, if any, Italy will join, but it's generally agreed she is likely to follow the precedent set by other nations and make her decisions solely on the basis of Italian national interest.

DECEMBER 25, 1939

Tonight I've been having dinner with English friends in London. We talked of the war. We remarked that fewer people were attending religious services these days. Many people prayed before the war came but now many of them seem for the time being to have given up the practice. But there was agreement that the search for some spiritual existence and support was something to which men have always returned and to which they will return again.

One of the best-known economists in this country, Sir Arthur Salter, sees this war as a return to the days of mercenary soldiers, when the number of actual fighters was small when compared to the total population. In such a system it is the duty of the entire population to organize and produce for the fighting men. Sir Arthur points out in a recent article that war demands a new type of organizer and planner, the executive rather than the regulator; people of vision who can do more than merely produce regulations designed to prevent a repetition of mistakes made during the last war. He wants administrators and government officials who can say yes instead of merely searching the regulations to find a reason for saying no.

As I understand the argument of this British economist, he believes that the war cannot be won without a large measure of state socialism. There is need for planning as well as regulation. According to Salter, proper planning would have produced the necessary number of pit props for Britain's mines, which in turn would have saved more coal than can be saved through rationing regulations. Britain has tried to run its propaganda service on civil-service lines, a system which permits the individual to escape responsibility by simply noting the contents of a folder and referring it to someone else for decision. That someone else generally passes it on to another cvil servant, and the process which is called operating through normal channels is almost endless. The system works within a rigid framework. The rules are designed to perpetuate the system, and the individual, whatever his competence or ability, has little room for personal initiative or decision. The British civil service has generations of traditions behind it. It has grown gradually into a routine system of administration which in the days of peace proved itself to be honest, somewhat slow, but efficient. But there are many who believe that the system is not sufficiently flexible for wartime operation.

The full implication of the financial and economic agreement between Britain and France has not yet come to the surface, but it is quite clear that during the coming months some very careful negotiations will have to be carried out between the British government and British labor. In France prices are fixed, and so are wages. The civilian workman is under roughly the same control as the soldier. In Britain prices have gone up and wages have been increased, though not sufficiently to compensate for the increased cost of living. There have been conferences between French and British labor leaders, and some observers believe that the British government is preparing a lower-war-wages campaign, attempting to bring the British workingman into a system more like that existing in France. If the effort is made it will be a political move of the greatest delicacy and may or may not be quietly accepted by British workmen.

During the past few weeks the speeches of Labour leaders have been considerably more critical of the government than they were during the early weeks of the war, and if an effort is made to freeze wages without at the same time fixing prices, Britain may be faced with its first industrial crisis of the war. It's an exceedingly complex business and the answer will not be known for some time.

DECEMBER 31, 1939

Tonight Britain says farewell, without regret, to this year of grace nineteen hundred and thirty-nine. When the year began there seemed some reason for hope. Mr. Chamberlain was claiming that peace in our time was assured. He was preparing to go to Rome for conferences with Signor Mussolini. Editorial writers were telling us one year ago today that Britain had been near to war in 1938, but there were brighter prospects for 1939. The big news in London at this time last year was that Germany had decided to build more submarines; that she would seek parity with Britain. London papers told their readers that this action need cause no alarm. Germany was acting in accordance with existing treaties, and anyway she probably wanted more submarines to meet the threat of Russian naval expansion.

One year ago today many writers were predicting a year of peace and prosperity. The new year was greeted with horns, sirens, and bells. There were gay parties in London's hotels, and families were together. Mr. Douglas Fairbanks left London for New York. American ships were still sailing from British ports. Unemployed men hung a huge banner on a London monument, asking that they should not starve during the new year. Astrologers predicted a year of peace and prosperity. Of course, there was war news a year ago, but it all seemed very remote to Londoners. There were pictures of exploding mines in our papers, but they were halfway around the world—in the war between China and Japan. Franco's bombers raided Barcelona twice, Italian forces south of Lérida were forced to retreat; but even the war in Spain seemed remote. Britain watched it from the shelter of the policy of nonintervention. The first pictures of a Lockheed bomber ordered from the United States appeared in an afternoon paper just one year ago today. There were the usual advertisements of post-Christmas sales. Sympathy was expressed for the bank clerks who must work extra-hard at new year's time. There was no mention in the news of Finland or of Turkey. President Hacha of Czechoslovakia sent new year's greetings to King George VI. The weather was bitterly cold, but London prepared to meet the new year with as much hope and cheer as possible. Underneath the usual routine celebrations and rosy prophecies was the feeling that 1938 had been a year in which force had triumphed. A long line of broken treaties stretched through the year.

Less than three months after Munich the need for additional air-raid precautions was being stressed. Appeasement and rearmament appeared in the same speeches. There was the feeling that the flower of safety had been plucked from the nettle; but the nettle was still there. There was still talk of an early general election to permit the Tory party to cash in on the relief felt when war was averted in September. The end of 1939 finds Britain near the end of the fourth month of a war which has confounded the experts. Roughly, one million men are under arms in Britain and hundreds of thousands more will probably be asked to register on Tuesday of next week. Homes have been broken up by evacuation. The cost of this war cannot be conveyed by mere figures. Not only the bank clerks are working this year. There are tens of thousands of men and women manning searchlights and antiaircraft guns, fire engines and ambulances, all over Britain. Many businesses have been ruined. Prices continue to rise. There are no bright lights this year, and there will be no sirens or horns sounded at midnight tonight, less they be confused with air-raid warnings.

Londoners have learned not to be afraid of the dark. When war came last September, there was almost a sense of relief. The suspense of waiting was ended, but the waiting hasn't ended. The uncertainty remains, plus a large degree of boredom. There are still rumors of peace moves; this time from Rome. But few have hopes that they will succeed. The speculation at the beginning of 1940 is concerned with the duration of the war. The experts seem to have been reading their prophecies of a year ago. But they're very cautious. Some foresee victory during the coming year. But they are a minority. The fact is that prophecy at this time is futile. One can do no more than to sum up the position as it is at the beginning of the new year.

The Allied preparations for victory continue. Victory will be achieved only when persons able to speak for the Ger-

man people ask for an armistice. That will not happen until
conditions inside Germany are worse than they would be if
the Germans surrendered, or at least until the Germans believe that their lot would be improved by admitting defeat.
War must be made intolerable, and that presumably is to
be achieved by military action.

There is no evidence at the beginning of the new year
that the Allies contemplate a large-scale offensive in the
west. They haven't the men to throw away. Therefore, they
must concentrate on blockade, while continuing to explore
the possibilities of creating another military front. The opinion seems to be that an air offensive alone would not produce conclusive results. If the German fortress can't be
taken from the front, nor smashed from the air, it must be
starved out, but the economic experts point out that the
open back door to the east makes that difficult.

People here believe that the blockade will gradually drive
down the standard of living in Germany. But unless the war
is to be stretched out for years, the German people must be
convinced by diplomatic action and by propaganda that
they will be better off if they give in.

At the beginning of 1940, despite speeches and pamphlets
to the contrary, the position seems to be that they should
take who have the power. And they should keep who can.

This is the only opportunity I shall have to extend new
year's greetings to my friends at home. Here they are: the
new year is at the door, I wish for the stupid a little understanding, and for the understanding a little poetry. I wish
a heart for the rich, and a little bread for the poor. But
above all, I wish that we may blackguard each other as little
as possible during the new year.

Those words were written by a German, Heinrich Heine
—a great man—who died in 1856.

JANUARY 1, 1940

Our ex-office boy paid us a visit today. He sat there in my
office, enveloped in an overcoat three sizes too big, with the
pockets of his bandoleer stuffed with paper. He's been in
the Army for four months now—in the signalers. In his own
words, he has spent most of the time just messing about.
At peeling potatoes he's an expert, but approaches the task
with a certain lack of sympathy. He's convinced that it takes
a long time to make a signaler. The other day he narrowly
avoided being made a batman—that is, an officer's servant—
and he's very pleased at having missed that opportunity.
Our ex-office boy reports that the food in the Army is good.
He also reports that during the past few months the lads
in his regiment have thought they were about to be sent to
India, Egypt, Palestine, France, and the north of England.
He says there's a lot of talk about Russia in barracks these
nights, but no one is anxious to go there. It's too cold. He
told me that the boys in his squad don't read the newspapers
very much. They have the idea that the same thing is
printed in different words, day after day, and they're not
sure what to believe. Our office boy belonged to the Terri-
torials and was called up a few days before war was declared.
He has a hearty contempt for those who have been conscripted, but thinks something may be made of them if the
old-timers have an opportunity to work on them a bit.

This young English boy, who used to lick stamps, operate
the telephone switchboard, and run errands, confessed that

he didn't think too much of the Army and would prefer to return to his old job. But when he left he said: "I suppose I'd best stop on until we get this mess cleared up."

There is much discussion here of assistance to Finland, but nothing new to report other than voluntary contributions. The military experts agree that assistance, if it's to be effective, must be immediate. But there's another consideration worth thinking about, and that is how long men's minds can retain the indignation created by events in Finland; how soon some new front-page development will drive it out of their minds; how long it will be before men's minds become callused. How many of us retain much of the sentiment or emotion felt over Austria, Abyssinia, Czechoslovakia, or Albania? Those places just aren't talked about any more. There seems to be in certain quarters an almost academic interest in how long the Finns can hold out. The indignation and the urge to act resulting from the invasion of Finland appear to be evaporating, although British sympathy for the Finns is strong.*

JANUARY 7, 1940

I should like to tell you about a man, a big man, six feet four inches of him, big and broad, with slender, athletic legs which give him a slightly top-heavy appearance. Legends without number have grown up about him. His name has a well-rounded sound calculated to inspire confidence, General Sir Edmund Ironside, Chief of the Imperial General Staff and Britain's number-one soldier. He is fifty-nine and

* Our sympathy for the Finns was strong too, but it evaporated in appropriations for "nonmilitary" loans, which could hardly be regarded as their most urgent need.

looks ten years younger. He is a storybook soldier, big, tough, brown-faced, gray hair and a little gray mustache. When you see him in a roomful of generals and admirals he seems to be looking over the heads of the lot of them.

Ironside was the first British soldier to step ashore in France in 1914. Later he commanded at Archangel and at Anatolia, spent two periods of service in India, commanded at Aldershot, and was Lieutenant of the Tower of London. Then a couple of years ago he was made Governor General of Gibraltar and people said he was through, for that job is generally given to generals who have been shelved. But he came back to be Inspector General of the Overseas Forces. He went to Burgos, to Paris, to Warsaw, and was finally given a big job, Chief of the Imperial General Staff.

General Ironside talks well and writes well. His summary of the Archangel campaign and his book on the Battle of Tannenberg are examples of clear, clean-cut, direct writing. He can act as interpreter in seven foreign languages and speaks half a dozen more well enough to get along with. His Russian is said to be flawless. But in normal conversation he prefers English and uses the direct, sometimes explosive, language understood by soldiers. He will answer questions with a single word and make his meaning perfectly clear.

The General has none too high an opinion of many politicians and he has been known to express that opinion without wasting words. A conversation between the Generals Ironside and Hugh Johnson would be worth hearing.

Big Bill Ironside, as he is called by the troops, works these days and nights behind a big desk at the War Office. Often he wears a tweed jacket and riding breeches, but always his brindle bulldog and a collection of brier pipes are near at hand. You can see him lunching almost any day at the United Service Club. I saw him there the other day, laughing and talking as though he were a country squire up from the country for the day. He is one of the few men I've ever seen who can smoke a really big cigar without looking just a little bit self-conscious. General Ironside handles a cigar the way an ordinary man does a cigarette. When he shakes hands with you you hope he is in a friendly mood.

No one can predict the future of this big, driving man, just as no one can be sure what part he played in the removal of Mr. Hore-Belisha from the War Office.* He hasn't had a great deal of publicity in this country, but he is certainly a leader of men, a soldier of soldiers who has demonstrated a willingness to take decisions without caring too much what the politicians will think.

He has power, likes action, and not least important he has a name—General Sir Edmund Ironside—a name that may be one to conjure with before this war is over.

MARCH 9, 1940

The spring diplomatic offensive is under way and there's certainly no indication that the British are pleased about it. Reports reaching London indicate that Russia, Finland, Sweden, Germany, and perhaps Italy are attempting to bring the war between Russia and Finland to an end. If they succeed the Allies will suffer a major diplomatic defeat and presumably Russia would then be free to increase her

* Ironside was made Commander of the Home Defense Force on May 27 and was put on the shelf on July 19—a lofty shelf, to be sure, with the rank of Field Marshal. And it is still true that no one can predict anyone's future; conceivably, Ironside might come back.

supplies to Germany. Of even greater importance would be
the fact that a settlement of the war in Finland would remove the political and moral grounds for an Allied thrust
against Russia in the middle east. If a negotiated settlement
is reached in Finland the Allies would then have to become
the aggressor in order to cripple or destroy Russian oil production. Since the beginning of the war in Finland, British
military experts have been pretty well agreed to this—that
the continuation of that war worked to the advantage of
France and Britain. There has been disagreement over the
amount and kind of aid that should be sent to Finland, but
the war itself, and its continuation, has been put down on
the asset side of the Allied ledger. If Finland is destroyed or
concludes a peace which leaves her in a position similar to
that occupied by Czechoslovakia after Munich, the Allied
task of winning the war becomes harder.

If the present negotiations, which seem to be scattered all
the way from Moscow to Rome, break down, it is thought
possible that Finland will make a direct appeal to Britain
and France for large-scale military aid. If that happens there
will be certainly a large body of opinion in this country and
in France in favor of granting that military aid. One thing
at least is clear from the confused welter of rumors and
counterrumors reaching London this morning. That is that
the diplomatic initiative remains in the hands of Germany
or Russia.

MARCH 10, 1940

The fact that there's been no large-scale American aid to
Finland has caused many Britishers to feel that earlier

American statements about selling small democracies down the river were just pious platitudes and nothing else. The change in the American neutrality law, permitting the export of arms, was welcome. But there is now a certain disposition to point out that American industries are making profit, and that a number of American plants are being expanded with British and French money. Occasionally one hears in London comments such as: "Protect us from a German victory and an American peace." Or: "The Americans wish us well, want us to win the war, but without interfering in any way with their business or profit." Many Englishmen, too, wonder about the repeated statements from your side of the Atlantic about an American participation in the peace. One of the attractions of war has always been that a belligerent, if he won, could make the peace. These Englishmen are wondering what America will contribute either to the war or to postwar security which will entitle them to a voice in the peace. They point out that they're never quite sure just what an American move or statement means. They recall President Roosevelt's speech about quarantining aggressors and ask how that fits in with the increasing supply of war materials to the Soviet Union. One columnist here in London the other day remarked that American sympathy for Finland was so great that it had caused a scramble to fill orders for the Soviet Union.

When Mr. Welles comes to Europe, Englishmen ask whether it reflects a real desire on the part of the President for firsthand information or whether it's just another move in the presidential campaign.

Mr. Joseph Kennedy, our Ambassador in London, comes back after a visit to the United States and is reported as saying that Americans fail to understand this war. The *Daily Express*, the biggest newspaper in Britain, suggests that Mr. Kennedy ought to explain it to them, since he's had an opportunity to study the war at first hand. Harold Nicolson, a Member of Parliament, writing in *The Spectator*, says that Mr. Kennedy conveyed to his countrymen a rather pessimistic view of the Allied prospects. Mr. Nicolson continues: "Were I to frequent only those circles in which Mr. Kennedy is so welcome a guest, I also should have long periods of gloom."

Our Ambassador in London will be welcomed by the Anglo-American colony, the native or unhyphenated rich, who hope that he may be bringing with him a little raft of appeasement on which they can float for a year or two longer. He will be welcomed, of course, by the bankers, the knights and baronets, the shiver-sisters of Mayfair and the wobble-boys of Whitehall, says Mr. Nicolson in his article in *The Spectator*. He goes on to say that a welcome will also be extended by the peace-pledge union, the friends of Herr von Ribbentrop, and the members of former pro-Nazi organizations. Mr. Nicolson anticipates that even Mr. Maisky, the Soviet Ambassador, will be glad to see Mr. Kennedy's return.

There is no doubt that a considerable number of people over here have resented Mr. Kennedy's utterances concerning the war. The British aren't accustomed to ambassadors expressing their frank opinions on international affairs in public—it isn't in the British tradition.

There's a feeling over here that our press at home has made too much of the search of American mails and perhaps too little of increased exports to neutral countries adjoining Germany. American talk of a negotiated peace sounds strange to many Englishmen, because they maintain that sincere and honest efforts were made to negotiate a peace before the war started. Any peace negotiated with the present German government, they say, would be something in the nature of a supercolossal Munich, and they haven't forgotten how roundly they were censured by Americans for that attempt at negotiations.

American assistance and support, economic and moral, are welcomed in Britain, but advice as to how the war should be conducted or how the peace should be made is distinctly less welcome. And so there are many people over here who foresee a certain amount of friction with the United States during the coming months. I don't want to exaggerate the importance of this development or the amount of concern it is causing in London, but it's impossible to ignore or fail to report such a trend of opinion when the signposts are so clearly marked.

MARCH 22, 1940

Good Friday in London was quiet. The English insist upon their holidays even in wartime, and today all of them who could have gone to the country, not to return until Tuesday of next week. For weeks past, English friends have been talking of little quiet villages in the country where there are no telephones and where the blackout has always been a normal state of affairs. They've been saving their gasoline coupons for the trip and the big exodus started this morning. The volume of railroad traffic was about normal for the Easter holiday period, but it included troops on leave and parents visiting their children in the country, as well as holidaymakers. Less than half the usual number of cars were on the road, but the number of bicycles has increased.

Here in London many streets were practically deserted. Both the Admiralty and the War Office showed less outward sign of activity, but the Air Ministry seemed busy as usual. There were long services in Westminster Abbey and the bells of St. Martin's-in-the-Fields echoed through streets that were nearly as empty as they are on a midsummer Sunday morning. While some prayed, others attended the traditional fair on Hampstead Heath, and the fair this year is complete with merry-go-rounds, fortunetellers, and all the trimmings. In most of the parks of London the crocuses are out in full strength, looking like brightly painted toy soldiers marching through a green meadow.

Strangely enough, Good Friday in London this year seems less tense and worried than it did on the same day last year. When Signor Mussolini chose Good Friday for the absorption of Albania, people were asking, "Will it be war?" News and rumor came pouring into London by wireless and telephone. Today nothing has happened to disturb the surface calm of wartime London.

APRIL 7, 1940

I want to tell you something about the new weapon being used in this war. It is in the opinion of many military correspondents the most powerful weapon that has come into being since the armored tank in 1916. The results achieved by this new weapon are already incalculable. When the full story of the German smash into Poland is written, this latest addition to the arsenal of war will receive much credit for the co-ordination of widely separated units both on the ground and in the air. The new weapon is radio. Bombing planes ride radio beams to their objectives. Spies transmit information in code by radio. Tanks go into action with their radio equipment keeping them in constant touch with aircraft and batteries. In the last war whole divisions were decimated because it required as much as five hours for orders to travel eight miles. Telephone lines, no matter how deeply buried in the ground, were generally cut in the first bombardment. Today short-wave transmitters keep troops in the field in constant and immediate touch with head-quarters. Today soldiers underground with only a worm's-eye view of the war listen to the radio to find out how the war is going.

But the home front is really the place where this two-edged weapon of attack and defense comes into its own. It's used to bolster morale and to give encouragement at home and to incite enemy civilians to revolution. It threatens or tries to reason with the enemy, debunk his propaganda. It tells the farmer how to get government seed and when to spray his apple trees. Occasionally it devotes a little time to educating children in the country who are without schools. The real objective of broadcasting into enemy countries is to hack away at civilian morale, undermine the will to fight, create doubts as to the honesty and integrity of national leaders, emphasize and exaggerate social and economic in-equalities, boast of your own achievements while pointing out that the enemy is without hope and fights for an un-worthy cause.

Every night, several times a night, Lord Haw-Haw, the English-speaking commentator from Hamburg, talks to millions of Britishers. He threatens, cajoles, and pleads. Each night he takes millions of British listeners by the ears and turns their eyes toward the less favorable aspects of British life: unemployment, profiteering, malnutrition, India, and all the rest. Each time he creates a doubt in the mind of a listener, he wins a victory. The British began by ridiculing him and are now taking him a little more seriously. No effort has been made to prevent people listening to him, but the British radio answers him, pointing out false statements and conducting what might be termed a sales-resistance campaign, for ideas as well as more tangible commodities can be sold by radio.

Tonight in every belligerent capital dozens of officials are listening to and recording news and propaganda broadcasts from all over the world. The British alone produce enough reports of foreign broadcasts to fill eight average-size novels every twenty-four hours. It is easier and quicker to appreciate changes in policy and propaganda by listening than it is by reading. Don't get the idea that radio is used by governments at war as of interest only to broadcasters or the people who want to be entertained. Military leaders must always be concerned about the morale of the civilian population at home. Most of you are familiar with the German explanations that Allied propaganda plus the stab in the back brought about Germany's defeat in the last war. Radio in Europe today, in addition to its purely military uses, is just about the finest back-stabbing weapon that could be placed in the hands of a Minister of Propaganda or Information.

If you believe that this war will be decided on the home front, then you must believe that radio used as an instrument of war is one of the most powerful weapons a nation possesses. If you believe, as I do, that this war is being fought for the control of men's minds, it is clear that radio will be a deciding factor. As employed by belligerent nations, it is the lash driving millions of questioning people backward toward an uncertain future. Truly there is danger in the air in Europe today, and the danger is not alone from bombing planes.

III

April 9 to May 8, 1940

APRIL 9, 1940. *Germany invades Denmark and Norway by air, sea, and land. The Danes capitulate. The Norwegians resist. German troops land at Norwegian port of Narvik above the Arctic Circle and two British destroyers are sunk.*

APRIL 10. *Belgium rejects British offer of "preventive aid."*

APRIL 13. *British war vessels attack Narvik, destroy or disable seven German cruisers, and clear harbor of most German craft.*

APRIL 15. *British fail to land troops at Narvik.*

APRIL 21. *Allied troops land at Namsos.*

MAY 3. *Allied evacuation of Norway continues and Colonel O. B. Getz, Norwegian commander, asks for an armistice and peace negotiations.*

MAY 7. *Prime Minister Chamberlain tells House of Commons that the Allied failure in Norway was due to two factors: "first of all, our inability to secure aerodromes from which we could operate our fighters, and, second, the rapid arrival of German reinforcements."*

MAY 8. *The House of Commons gives Chamberlain government a 281–200 vote of confidence, with at least 130 Conservatives abstaining.*

WAR IN NORWAY

APRIL 8, 1940

Not for a long time has London had a day like today. That something-is-going-to-happen atmosphere that marked the early days of the war has returned. Gas masks, pretty well discarded during recent months, began to appear again this afternoon. The day's news, while it may not herald the beginning of a *Blitzkrieg*, certainly marked the end of the winter-long *Sitzkrieg*. The British press and radio are unanimous in approving the mining of Norwegian territorial waters. The Norwegians have protested. If Norway sweeps up the mine fields, Britain will plant them again. If the Germans try to clear a channel or initiate a naval engagement, well, nothing would please the British more. One thing is certain, and that is no matter how strongly Norway or any other neutral protests, the British aren't going to pick up those mines and bring them home again.

No one here seems to be particularly worried about the outcome of this new phase of the war. It's a job for the Navy and the confidence of the British in their Navy is supreme. It is admitted here that Britain has violated international law and that she had signed an agreement with Norway permitting that country to trade freely with Germany. But the British maintain that they had sufficient provocation for the action. They deny that the Allies desire to extend the war to Scandinavia. Norway, they say, did not defend her neutrality with sufficient vigor—and that's that.

This is not the first violation of neutral sovereignty, nor is it likely to be the last. Earlier wars were like boxing—hitting only with the fists and above the belt. This one is rapidly reaching the point where nothing is barred—teeth, feet, heads, toes, and fingers will be used by all belligerents; anything to get at a vulnerable part of the opponent's anatomy.

According to the latest reports received in London, a considerable German naval force, estimated at between ninety and one hundred ships, is moving out of the Baltic. This force is said to be composed mainly of mine sweepers and trawlers. Unofficially London claims that British submarines have accounted for two German ships today—a 12,000-ton tanker and a troop ship believed to have been carrying three thousand men; half of them were drowned. A German merchantman and a U-boat are also believed to have been accounted for. All these naval actions took place in or near Norwegian waters. There are unconfirmed rumors that Berlin has told Norway to sweep up those Allied mines or suffer the consequences. There are also rumors that the British fleet has entered the Baltic. But whether it has or not, and probably it hasn't, German planes bombed Scapa Flow again tonight.

Today in the British Foreign Office—that big, gray smoke-grimed building in Downing Street, just opposite Mr. Chamberlain's residence—eight British ambassadors have been meeting with Lord Halifax. The results of these talks with Britain's diplomats from Russia, Italy, and the Balkans will probably be conveyed to the House of Commons in its secret session on Thursday. But it is safe to assume that each man is asking for pretty much the same thing—more loans, more trade, more propaganda for the country to which he is accredited. Buy up the Balkans. If they're determined to remain neutral, Britain must do everything possible to prevent them from supplying Germany with goods. The doing of that will put a tremendous strain upon British economy, and even if it can be done, the price must be paid by a lowering of the standard of living of the masses of this country.

While the diplomats talk and the Navy stands guard over its new mine fields, a Gallup survey claims that the British public would prefer Mr. Anthony Eden above all others as Prime Minister if Mr. Chamberlain should retire. Winston Churchill is a close second, with Lord Halifax third. Clement Attlee, leader of the opposition, and Mr. David Lloyd George follow in that order. This survey which claims to be an accurate cross section shows that during the last year Churchill has gained and Eden has lost. The young ex-Foreign Secretary who has been cautious and correct since he left office leads Mr. Churchill by only 3% as the nation's favorite successor to Neville Chamberlain.

[*That night the German expeditionary force landed in Norway.*]

APRIL 9, 1940

I was in the House of Commons this afternoon, and it was a tense and expectant House. Members became a little impatient as the big clock above the Speaker's chair ticked off the minutes, while no less than one hundred and eleven questions were answered by various Cabinet ministers. Everyone wanted to hear the Prime Minister. When Mr. Chamberlain rose briskly to his feet, silence settled over the House. He began by quoting, almost with satisfaction, from his speech made at the end of the Finnish war, in which he predicted that the policy of Sweden and Norway would not in the end save them from aggression.

The Prime Minister went on to say that the Allies were going to the assistance of Norway and that heavy units of the fleet were now at sea. The speech was brief and added nothing to reports that had been published. The Prime Minister proved to his own satisfaction, and apparently to the satisfaction of the House as well, that the German smash into Denmark and Norway was well under way before the Allies began laying mines in the Norwegian waters. No one suggested the possibility that the Germans, through clever intelligence work, may have had advance information concerning Allied moves. The opposition leaders expressed sympathy for the people of Denmark and Norway and hoped that Allied aid would be both prompt and effective. The debate that followed, if it can be called a debate, was noisy and inconclusive; one member suggesting that the matter should be referred to the League of Nations was howled down. Another wanting to advocate an immediate and complete change of government was swamped by a wave of shouting and cries of "order, order" and "sit down." Still another back-bencher wanted to make a speech about Japanese aggression in China—at least I think that's what he wanted to talk about. He had no chance at all. One question as to why the Germans were able to effect a landing in the north of Norway when British naval patrols were out, and when Britain claims control of the sea, met with a caustic reply from the Prime Minister. He suggested that the questioner restrain both his impatience and his criticism until the facts are known.

The debate was brief. The House didn't want to talk about anything except the war against Germany and there was nothing to be said about that after the Prime Minister's speech. Members were inclined to be bellicose and at times unruly. They clearly wanted a victory, not lengthy discussion. There was no drama in the Commons this afternoon comparable with that involved in the announcement of Mr. Chamberlain's flight to Munich. No parliamentary leader attacked the government. The House approved overwhelmingly of the decision to aid Norway and appeared willing to wait for news as to just how that was going to be done. But there were many indications, both in the House and in the lobbies afterward, that Parliament expects prompt and decisive action. If it should be said of Norway, as it was of Finland, that Allied help was too little and too late, there would be changes in the political leadership of this country.

Military correspondents in London do not underestimate the difficulty involved in the landing of an Allied expeditionary force in Norway. Such an operation presents one of the most difficult of all military maneuvers, since it involves the combined operation of the Army, Navy, and Air Force. Staff work and weather conditions will probably be the determining factors, when and if a British expeditionary force is dispatched. It is well to remember that though there is discussion of the many problems involved in connection with the landing of an Allied force in Norway there is no official indication that such a force is on the way. The belief that Allied troops are en route to Norway is based mainly upon the assumption that if Britain and France were confident that they could transport and maintain an expeditionary force of more than 100,000 men in Finland they should be able with greater ease to carry out a similar undertaking in Norway.

It is admitted in London that the German occupation of Denmark will reduce Britain's supplies of agricultural products, particularly butter and bacon. But the Minister of Food has pointed out that there are sufficient reserve stores available to prevent a shortage.

Comment from Paris states that Germany's difficulties will begin as soon as she has seized Denmark's present supplies, since the Allied blockade will immediately begin to cripple that country's agriculture and industry. Certain neutral writers, particularly in Holland, condemn the Allies for not foreseeing and forestalling the German action in Scandinavia. The opinion in Holland seems to be that it is now or never. The western powers must show that their promises to help the smaller states are something more than mere newspaper talk. Mr. Menzies, the Australian Prime Minister, believes that Germany has purchased a small, immediate gain at the price of an increasing antagonism throughout the civilized world.

And so at one o'clock in the morning London does not know what steps have been taken to assist Norway, does not know which of the many rumors of naval actions in the stormy waters of the North Sea off the coast of Norway should be believed. But the British are confident of their Navy and believe that Mr. Churchill will have good news for them before many hours have passed.

APRIL 11, 1940

Mr. Winston Churchill left the famous Map Room at the Admiralty and went to the House of Commons this afternoon to tell the House and the world how the war at sea is getting on. His arrival in the packed House of Commons was greeted by that low-pitched roar reserved by the House for Ministers who enjoy the confidence and respect of all political parties. Mr. Churchill was tired, his face expressionless, as he walked down to his seat beside the Prime Minister. He rubbed his eyes, whispered a few words to Mr. Chamberlain, put on his spectacles, and began a speech which was to last for nearly an hour and ten minutes.

It was a mixture of oratory, confidential asides, sarcasms, and humor. Before Mr. Churchill arrived there was an air of exaggerated casualness in the House, as though members were determined not to display by words or facial expression their uncertainty and desire for news. But from the moment Mr. Churchill began to speak he held the attention of the House in a steady grip. He spoke in a rather hesitating manner and his fatigue was reflected in his frequent search for the right word. When he lowered his voice the House literally leaned toward him and when he wanted a laugh he got it—as when he spoke of the fact that the leader of the opposition had unfortunately missed an air raid while visiting Scapa; or again when he spoke of the German plunder and pillage of small nations, especially their food; or yet again when he spoke of the necessity for further air raids on Scapa Flow in order that British gunners might get more practice. It was a fighting speech, full of confidence but with a warning that heavy blows are to be expected. When he spoke of dive bombing, his left hand was the German cruiser and his descending right hand the British bomber. On one occasion he had difficulty reading his notes and had to change to another pair of spectacles. One had the feeling that nearly everyone in the House wanted to help him.

Mr. Churchill today was a combination of orator, actor, elder statesman, and fighting prophet. He was more than that. He was the man who for five years had sat in his corner seat beneath the gangway, a political exile, while he uttered warnings of increasing German might as he watched the big clock above the Speaker's chair tick off what he believed to be missed opportunities.

Mr. Churchill today was also a reporter with an exclusive story to tell, and, always a brilliant journalist, he told it well. He talked not only of fighting; he warned the small neutrals that they might suffer the fate of Norway and Denmark if they didn't come to an understanding with the Allies now.

The House of Commons liked Mr. Churchill's speech. It may be said that he didn't give them very much information, but he told them why on certain occasions the information cannot be given. It was certainly the most brilliant effort seen in the House of Commons since the war started. Here is a quick summary of what he told them:

He said that since yesterday sea and air fighting had been continued night and day without a stop and is now going on. It is widely dispersed but nonetheless a general action between a large number of German ships and aircraft and such forces as we were able to bring to bear. He said, "We have not recaptured those ports on the Norwegian coast. These rumors from neutral sources have been given currency but the House has read a great deal of truth and more that is not true in the last few days." On Tuesday afternoon the British fleet was attacked continuously by German aircraft; two cruisers, slightly damaged, but this did not interfere with their work. One large bomb struck the flagship *Rodney* but her heavy armor deflected the blow. That announcement was greeted with cheers because the British had been somewhat concerned about the effect of air bombing against their heavy capital ships.

He went on to say that far to the north of Narvik, at daybreak Tuesday morning, the *Renown* perceived the German cruiser *Scharnhorst* and another vessel of the *Hipper* class. Gales were blowing furiously and the *Renown* opened fire at 18,000 yards. The action was broken off at 29,000 yards after the *Hipper*-class cruiser had thrown a smoke screen for the protection of the *Scharnhorst*. He also said that "we are at this moment in occupation of the Faeroe Islands which belong to Denmark. The people," said Mr. Churchill, "received us very warmly and we shall establish ourselves there until the time when they will be handed back to Denmark."

The First Lord also announced that all German ships in the Skagerrak and Kattegat will be sunk and by night all ships will be sunk as opportunity serves. "We are not going to allow the German navy to supply her armies across these waters with impunity," and he said, "Herr Hitler has committed a grave strategic error in extending the war so far to the north and forcing the Scandinavian people out of their traditional attitude of neutrality."

APRIL 22, 1940

The headlines tell us that the British Expeditionary Force

has crossed Norway, is on the Oslo front, and has recaptured Elverum and Hamar. That is what the headlines say. But the stories underneath are made up of unconfirmed reports that have traveled circuitous routes to provide their unsubstantial support for optimistic headlines. The British think their troops in Norway are doing well, but they have no news of how the fighting is going at Narvik, Namsos, or anywhere else. They know that the Norwegian campaign is important. Its outcome may determine both Italian and Russian policy as well as the uncertain future of the Reynaud government. If Norway lives it will strengthen the determination of the other small neutrals to fight for their lives. The British people have been told that Hitler has made a first-class blunder, that he has come out from his protecting wall of the Siegfried Line and the small neutrals to where he can be hit. Germany has scored an unending succession of diplomatic triumphs and surprises, but it is a question of force now. As one London paper puts it, the Allies are not judged by their virtues nor Nazi Germany by her vices. Power is the single test. British spokesmen have welcomed the creation of this new theater of war, and the news of the action at sea and in the air has been encouraging, but most people would be grateful for a little more news, whether it is encouraging or not.

Many London publicists are beginning to suspect that the Germans sent a telegraphic Quisling into Britain last week in the form of reports from Stockholm asserting that Allied troops have retaken Bergen and Trondheim. Now if it seems strange to find German sources putting out stories of Allied successes, just remember what happened during the Polish campaign when the German radio claiming to be British broadcast promises of the immediate arrival of thousands of British planes and troops for the relief of Poland. There can be no question that the handling by press and radio in this country of the news from Norway during the past ten days has undermined the confidence of a considerable section of the British public in the integrity and the accuracy of its news sources. It is only fair to point out that the press and radio over here are helpless. They begged the Admiralty and the War Office for confirmation or denial and got neither. Departmental and personal jealousies have not been entirely eliminated. There is no indication that the Ministry of Information has established any effective degree of control over the issuance of news or denials. The fighting services still have the whip hand and apparently are not concerned about, or are not aware of, the flood of disturbing statement and rumor reaching this country from abroad.

Don't misunderstand me. This is not a reporter's personal complaint. *The New Statesman* in its last issue asserts that sometimes America expects Britain to run a box-office war for the benefit of American correspondents. I am not complaining about either the absence of news or the way the war is being run. I am simply telling you that a significant proportion of thoughtful Englishmen are concerned about the manner in which news is given or not given to the British public. They are worried lest the repeated issuance of news, later proved to be false, may create an unhealthy amount of skepticism on the home front, and believe me, the home front is going to be increasingly important as this war progresses.

There are many exiles scattered about Europe, men without countries, many of them having sought refuge in half

a dozen nations during the past five years. They have been
living just one jump ahead of the concentration camp, and
now considerable numbers are to find a home in intern-
ment camps because they can't prove that they have no
connection with Germany. The feeling is growing all over
Europe that it is wiser to throw a hundred innocent men in
jail than that one Nazi agent be allowed to operate dis-
guised as a refugee.

Mr. Harold Nicolson, in this week's *Spectator*, points an
accusing pen at British subjects who have sought refuge
from chaos in America. He speaks particularly of four brilliant and promising English writers now in America, W. H.
Auden, Christopher Isherwood, Aldous Huxley, and Gerald
Heard. Mr. Nicolson asserts that his quarrel with these four
horsemen of the Apocalypse who have dismounted and led
their horses back into the distant Hollywood stable is that
they came out of their ivory towers when the sun of June
was upon the meadows and then retreated to them when
the winds of autumn began to howl. Mr. Nicolson is writing about men who have been his friends, and his words
may be taken as another indication of an attitude which
most neutral observers here believe to be increasing in
strength and vigor. That attitude is those who are not for
us are against us.

MAY 2, 1940

The British withdrawal from southern Norway does not
mean the end of the Norwegian campaign, merely a new
phase. The objectives of the first phase have been attained.
That's what an officially inspired statement, issued after Mr.

Chamberlain's speech, declares. The statement goes on to claim that Hitler has lost one third of his fleet and has been forced to pour perhaps one hundred thousand men into Norway, and German losses in both material and men have been much heavier than those of the Allies. It is pointed out that the British evacuation was carried out in an orderly and successful manner. Narvik and other places on the coast are still in British hands and will be held. It is also claimed that the balance of advantage still lies with the Allies.

I was in the House of Commons this afternoon when Mr. Chamberlain made his statement and did not get the impression that members of that body shared the optimistic interpretation of the official statement. The Prime Minister began by recounting the history of Norwegian developments. He said that the expeditionary force prepared for service in Finland had been dispersed, but that a small force had been kept in readiness to take over ports on the west coast of Norway. He then told of the British landings at various points on the Norwegian coast, including those north and south of Trondheim, because, he said, the Allies had realized the importance of taking that city. When Mr. Chamberlain remarked that it was obviously impossible for him to discuss details of the fighting many members thought that was all the information they were going to get, but he went on in a quiet, level voice to announce that British troops had been withdrawn from Aandalsnes and the area south of Trondheim. The Prime Minister gave no figures of British casualties in Norway, but he indicated that they were not unduly heavy considering the size of the operations.

A number of reasons were advanced for the British withdrawal—the inadequacy of docking facilities had made it impossible to land heavy guns and tanks. The Germans had been able to reinforce their troops more quickly and effectively than the Allies and, above everything else, he gave German air superiority as the reason for the withdrawal. Mr. Chamberlain promised that the campaign in Norway would not become a side show, but he said that Britain did not propose to weaken her center by having too many troops sucked into the Norwegian campaign. Britain must guard against the possibility of an invasion of Belgium, of Holland, a thrust to the southeast, as well as the possibility of a lightning invasion of England. A statement that British and French warships were now on their way to Alexandria drew one of the few cheers of the afternoon. Mussolini's belligerent nonbelligerency may have influenced considerably the British decision not to become too heavily engaged in Norway.

When Mr. Chamberlain concluded his speech there was a dead, flat silence. The leaders of the opposition agreed to postpone their questions until the full debate on the war schedule for next week. All during the Prime Minister's speech, Mr. Winston Churchill slumped in his seat, playing with his fingers and watching the House and its reactions with great interest. You will want to know whether this British reverse is likely to bring down Mr. Chamberlain's government. It's too early to tell. Things happen slowly in British politics. Few would deny that dissatisfaction with the government has increased, but a change of government in this country requires two things: a crisis and a group of men ready and willing to take over the direction of the nation's affairs. That group of men has not yet been formed.

Many members of Parliament are discussing the possibility of an alternative government tonight and they will probably continue to do so throughout the week end. Much will depend upon the way the press handles the affair in the next two or three days and upon the temper of the House of Commons when it meets to debate the war on Tuesday. The future of this government rests largely in the rather pudgy hands of Winston Churchill. If he should openly blame the political leadership of the country for the reverse in Norway, Mr. Chamberlain's government might be forced to resign. So far, there is no indication that the First Sea Lord contemplates such action. There is no obvious ready-made alternative to the present government and, so long as there is no split in the War Cabinet, Mr. Chamberlain's government is in no immediate danger. The British are not in the habit of overthrowing governments because of military defeats. If this government falls, it will be because Parliament and the people are convinced that it has not been sufficiently resolute or determined in forging the men, money, and materials of this country into one fist to smite the Germans.

Next week's debate on the conduct of the war will be the most critical in the nine months of this war. Much political maneuvering will go on within the next few days, but if Mr. Churchill and the other members of the War Cabinet stand with the Prime Minister there will be no change. So far, there has been no comment, official or otherwise, of the effect of today's announcement on the Norwegian government and army. Reports reaching London from Switzerland say that the Swiss are unable to understand why the Allies failed to anticipate lightning retaliation by the Germans when the Navy planted its mine fields off the coast of Norway. The Swiss seem to feel that the Allies will continue to be caught unawares by swift German moves until they come to appreciate and anticipate the dynamic character of national socialism.

May 10 to June 16, 1940

MAY 10, 1940. At 5 A.M., without warning, German troops cross the Belgian, Luxembourg, and Netherlands boundaries. Air, sea, and land forces go into action; also parachute troops.

MAY 11. Chamberlain government resigns and Winston Churchill becomes Prime Minister, retaining Halifax as Foreign Secretary, making Chamberlain Lord President of the Council, and taking into the Cabinet Labour members of Parliament who had always refused to support Chamberlain.

Foreign Minister Arita of Japan announces that his country will not permit the Netherlands Indies to change hands.

MAY 13. As German troops continue to sweep across Holland and Belgium, Queen Wilhelmina and the Dutch royal family flee from The Hague to London on two British destroyers.

The British House of Commons upholds the new Churchill Cabinet by a vote of 318–0 as Churchill declares, "I have nothing to offer but blood, toil, tears, and sweat. We have before us an ordeal of the most grievous kind. We have before us many, many months of struggle and suffering. You ask, what is our policy? I say it is to wage war by land, sea, and air."

MAY 14. General Winkelman, Dutch Commander in Chief, capitulates to Germany.

MAY 16. German troops pass Sedan.

MAY 18. German troops occupy Antwerp and reach the Aisne River in France. Premier Reynaud appoints Marshal Pétain Vice-Premier.

MAY 19. General Weygand succeeds General Gamelin as French chief of staff.

MAY 20. Units of the British Expeditionary Force begin to retreat through Belgium ports as German troops continue their sweep across Belgium and France.

MAY 21. A German army captures Amiens on the Somme and advances to Abbeville, thus cutting off French and Belgian armies to the north and forcing them toward the Channel.

MAY 22. British Parliament passes Emergency Powers Defense Act giving the Churchill Cabinet unlimited power to direct the nation's war effort.

MAY 23. German troops reach the Channel port of Boulogne.

MAY 28. King Leopold surrenders his army of 500,000 men to the Germans.

MAY 29. British forces in Flanders begin large-scale evacuation from Dunkerque.

JUNE 4. The Allies abandon Dunkerque. The British Admiralty announces over 335,000 men saved. Churchill announces more than 30,000 killed, wounded, or missing. The Germans claim 40,000 prisoners. Churchill admits loss of nearly 1000 guns and all transport and armored vehicles. He pledges, "We shall never surrender."

JUNE 9. German troops come within 35 miles of Paris.

JUNE 10. Foreign Minister Ciano announces that, as of June 11, Italy would consider itself at war with France. President Roosevelt says, "The hand that held the dagger has stuck it into the back of its neighbor."

JUNE 12. The French government informs the German High Command through Ambassador Bullitt that Paris is an open city and will not be defended.

JUNE 14. German troops enter Paris as French shift their government from Tours to Bordeaux.

JUNE 16. Premier Reynaud resigns as French Premier and is succeeded by Marshal Pétain with General Weygand as Vice-Premier.

WAR IN THE WEST

[*The German attack on the Netherlands and Belgium be-*
gan before daylight on May 10. For four days news of the
progress of that attack left little room for anything else; the
story is resumed when people in western Europe first began
to have time to think and when Britain had installed a new
all-party government.]

MAY 14, 1940

The fighting in Holland has apparently ceased, with the
exception of the province of Zeeland. This information is
contained in broadcasts issued from Hilversum, and an official communiqué from British General Headquarters simply states that the move of the British Expeditionary Force
has proceeded according to plan and contact with the enemy
has been maintained throughout the day.

The speed of the German drive into Belgium has surprised most of the unofficial military experts in London. But
the German objectives are not yet definitely established.
When von Moltke pulled the trigger of the Kaiser's big war
machine in 1914 the direction was Paris and the objective
the destruction of the Allied field army. It is felt here that
Hitler's orders may have been different—that his order of
the day may have said: "Direction, England—objective,

Allied air bases." The seizure of the Dutch and Belgian ports will provide Germany with the necessary bases for attack against English ports and airdromes. The German radio is already threatening such action. The British are concerned not only about bombing but about parachute troops. Tonight Anthony Eden, the new War Minister, broadcast an appeal for local defense volunteers. They are to report to the nearest police station, will be issued uniforms and arms, and will in fact be a part-time home-defense army. Bicycle clubs are reported to be organizing observation patrols to watch for parachutists, particularly at dawn and dusk.

Reports from East Anglia and the east coast state that farmers are oiling up their fowling pieces, preparing to receive what they call "these umbrella men."

Britain is pledged to victory, victory at all costs, but it is widely felt here that the next two months must be devoted to avoiding defeat and if that can be done the drive for victory will come later. From the very beginning of this new campaign on Europe's traditional battleground there has been no tendency here to underrate the difficulties or create hopes of an early or easy victory. There is no repetition of the easy optimism that characterized the early days of the fighting in Norway.

Many people believe that Mr. Chamberlain's government made the mistake of asking too little rather than too much of the people of this country. They seem now to be realizing that the casual luxury phase of the war has ended, that long-range economic warfare and the mighty British fleet are not alone sufficient to win victory or avoid defeat. They have been told that dark days are ahead. Bad news has come out of Flanders before. There are no surface indications that these people want to draw back from the danger and misery that lie ahead. They have a new leadership and, while politics has not been entirely abandoned, an impressive degree of unity has been achieved.

The additional Cabinet appointments announced tonight represent in the main a trading of jobs amongst established politicians, but that's not surprising. The business of governing has been traditionally confined to a limited group of men in this country. Once a man is established in politics, it seems to be difficult for him to lose his position.

To me, one of the most interesting things about Mr. Churchill's Cabinet is this: he appears to be putting outstanding critics in positions where they must by their deeds refute their own criticism. Attlee and Greenwood have been demanding a small War Cabinet. Now they're in a small War Cabinet. Herbert Morrison led the attack against the Ministry of Supply and now he's the new Minister of Supply. Duff Cooper was one of the most persistent critics of the Ministry of Information. And now he has the job of running Britain's propaganda machine. Mr. A. V. Alexander has been a persistent critic of the Admiralty, so Mr. Churchill turns the Navy over to him. Sir John Simon has for many years fancied himself as a future Prime Minister and Mr. Churchill sends him to the House of Lords with a nice salary and thereby ends his hopes of leading the House of Commons. And Lord Beaverbrook, who has been shouting for years in big type for airplanes and more airplanes, is made Minister for Aircraft Production.

Belgian officials have stated today that the capital is in no danger, but I am told that most if not all of the British correspondents have left Brussels.

MAY 21, 1940

News from the front reaches Britain through terse and laconic communiqués issued from the headquarters of the French and British armies in the field. These are supplemented by occasional revelations of a high Army officer in the confidence of the War Office, who is known as a military spokesman. This gentleman is well accustomed to handling the press and when he meets them gives a kind of summary of Allied operations and for anything up to half an hour answers questions, generally with a negative.

The British military spokesman today summed up the position as follows: at the moment the situation is more confused than ever. The German effort is directed west and north with the twofold object, that of capturing the Channel ports and cutting off the northern armies of Belgium and Great Britain. The Germans have reached Amiens but in what force or with what effect is not yet known. There is no confirmation here of the German claim that Abbeville has been reached.

A great many of these forward sallies in Hitler's new type of warfare are made with marauding tanks, often with the object of terrorizing the country into the belief that a mighty German army is on top of them. Actually, there may be no more than a dozen tanks operating as a squadron or regiment of cavalry used to function in the days of horse warfare. Some of these tanks are very big. The British have big tanks too, bigger than anything so far seen in the German ranks. The *Daily Telegraph* reports that Mr. Peter Bennett, Director General of Tanks and Transport, described the new eighty-ton tanks of the British Army which are now in course of production. It is felt that when these monsters meet the Germans the equilibrium will be restored.

In the south the French are holding firm and at many places well within the German advance lines units of the French army are fighting magnificently. Behind the whole front, the military spokesman said the Royal Air Force was harassing the German communications and destroying German army supplies, particularly oil and gasoline.

The Germans, according to this officer, got nothing from Holland and it was British demolition parties who blew up key supply points and particularly the huge gasoline storage yards of the big oil companies.

The military spokesman concluded by explaining that the big scare over the cessation of telephone communication between the British and French capitals last night was next door to nonsense. What had happened was that the government had taken over the telegraph lines for official business. Apparently it intends to reserve them for such business from now on, and those who have private or commercial affairs to discuss will have great difficulty obtaining transmission.

One thing is becoming increasingly clear in London, and that is the objective of the German drive. It is to roll up the British right flank, pin the British and Belgians against the coast, and then give them the alternative of surrender, annihilation, or attempted evacuation by sea under German guns and German bombers. The British have been told repeatedly that Germany has risked all in an effort to win quickly. The speed of the German advance has staggered military experts here, but let me say again there is no panic.

There is a feeling of surprise and bewilderment, a realization that the German bid for victory is directed by unorthodox minds, willing to attempt the impossible, and favored so far by incredible luck. No rain in Poland, storms off the Norwegian coast, and now by ten days of clear weather and moonlit nights.

The news from France is not creating any panic in this country, but an air of urgency is developing. Tolerance is decreasing and the temperature is rising. The Royal Air Force is calling up deferred men, that is, men who have registered and who have not yet actually started training. The number of reserved occupations, jobs that freed men from the draft, will probably be reduced.

Gun shops were raided by Scotland Yard this morning. Their stores of guns were removed. During most of the winter and spring this seemed an almost casual war as viewed from London. The British exhausted their vocabulary of condemnation, asserted that right was on their side, and seemed to feel that Germany could be strangled at long range without too much trouble. All that has changed. The change doesn't show itself in hysteria or patriotic outbursts. In fact, it would be hard to put into words this change that has taken place. To me it seems that this country is younger than it was ten days ago. There is more bitterness not only against the Germans, but against the men in this country who failed to realize the nature of the German threat, who failed to prepare to meet it, those who failed to drive the aircraft production at top speed in the days following Munich, those who starved the British Secret Service for funds. There is no more talk of peace aims, only talk of holding on, avoiding defeat, and then trying for victory.

Britain's Minister of Information, broadcasting tonight, admitted that the news was grave but gave no cause for panic. The French and British armies were intact and no heavy losses had been sustained. Mr. Duff Cooper warned against false and disturbing rumors and emphasized that the end of the battle is the thing that counts.

MAY 22, 1940

The British revolution, part of it at least, occurred today. It was a quiet revolution; no bloodshed, no crowds singing and marching in the streets. The scene was the House of Commons. The man who made the announcement didn't look like a revolutionary leader. There is nothing heroic about Clement Attlee as the new Lord Privy Seal. But he quietly informed the House today that the government was taking over complete control of all persons and all property. Not just some proper persons and some property, but everything. Control over all persons, rich or poor, employer or worker, man or woman, and all property. All of it—including the land. Men will work where and when and for such pay as the Minister of Labor may direct. Factories may be taken over. The excess-profits tax is to be 100%. Essential businesses operating at a loss will receive a subsidy. Over a wide field industry will be carried on for the community and not for private profit.

If you were an Englishman, then the government could take your car, your house, your factory, your bank account, everything you have, and it could tell you what kind of work you were to do and how much you would be paid for it—in fact, as an English friend remarked to me tonight, "The

government can now take over everything but your over-
draft at the bank and your debts. It can even tell your wife
what she is to do." All those things can be done, but it is
likely that only limited application will be given to this new
bill—at least for the time being.* The increased organization required will be enormous and can't be carried out in a
few days. But the fact remains that everything save conscience can now be conscripted in this country.

My own summary of today's speech by Mr. Attlee is this:
he said the situation is grave. Everyone knows the issues at
stake. We are free men fighting for our lives, and in order
that we may fight more effectively we must give up our
freedom.

The revolution announced today by that small man in
rather ill-fitting clothes and loose collar marked the course
along which Britain will travel. During most of the postwar
period this country has been ruled by men with extensive
stakes in the profits of industry, by an oligarchy which has
believed in its right to rule. Whether they have ruled well
or ill is not at this moment important. The remote past has
been blotted out by the news of yesterday. Britain now
places supreme control over the individual in the hands of
the government. It's a new government. Had the old government recognized the lateness of the hour, these new
powers might not have been necessary, but this country is
now united and it is important that a lifelong socialist introduced that revolutionary bill today.

It jarred the House of Commons, but it was accepted.
The bill passed both Houses of Parliament in just two hours
and thirty minutes. In terms of political procedure, Britain

* Eight months later, they were just beginning to apply it.

now becomes a totalitarian state, but her announced objectives differ drastically from those of other totalitarian states. I should like to repeat just one sentence from a talk given from here two weeks before war was declared: "The greatest threat of the totalitarian concept is that it forces those who fear it to imitate it."

MAY 23, 1940

The British Parliament in one hundred and sixty-three minutes yesterday swept away the freedom acquired in the last thousand years. Today the press of this country applauds the action. The *Daily Express* says Hitler started this war eight years ago; we start it today. The *Daily Mail* calls it a discipline act which will be eagerly accepted. The mouthpiece of the Socialist party, the *Daily Herald*, salutes the intelligence of the statesmen who introduced the bill. Now all are one: reactionaries and profit seekers are reduced to impotence, says the *Herald*. The conservative *Times* believes that Parliament has fulfilled the dearest wish of the people. The demand now is that the government, equipped with supreme power, shall begin to use it. Many men of twenty-four and twenty-five, although they registered months ago, have not yet been called up. The construction of buildings not essential to war work has been going on.

Some time will be required for these new regulations to begin operating, but the speed with which the government will take over the control of life and property in this country will probably be surprising to the British who are accustomed to a cumbersome, slow-moving government machine bound in red tape, formality, and tradition.

Today has brought little news of the fighting in France and Belgium. It is reported that both British and French tanks are engaged in heavy fighting near Cambrai and that the French have reached the outskirts of that city. In the area south of Arras in the direction of Amiens the mixup of German and Allied mechanized units continues. It is admitted that Germany's dynamite and incendiary squads are still running loose in Picardy, setting fire to textile towns, lace factories, and anything else that will burn. The last British communiqué says that enemy motorized units have reached the neighborhood of the coast.

Members of Parliament are beginning to ask questions about Ireland. They are disturbed by reports of underground Nazi agitation in Eire. So far M.P.s have refrained from asking too many questions, in view of Mr. De Valera's difficulties with the Irish Republican Army. But the reticence has now disappeared, and a deputation of Conservative members is to visit the Prime Minister to ask him what is being done to protect England's back door. Alarm is being expressed at the large number of German diplomats and newspapermen now stationed in Dublin. In the House of Commons this afternoon a number of questions will be asked about Ireland. There is a demand that pro-German Irishmen in Great Britain be interned. And members want to know whether the government has received any assurance from Dublin concerning the attitude Mr. De Valera's government will take in the event of an invasion. Lord Craigavon, the Premier of Northern Ireland, is in London, talking with Mr. Churchill today.

The temper of this country is changing rapidly. A few weeks ago German prisoners of war in this country were receiving packages of food and clothing from British civilians. German prisoners arriving in this country were greeted with silence or good-natured jests. But yesterday when twenty-two German airmen were landed at a southeast coast port, an angry crowd, including many women, shouted, "Shoot the murdering swine!"

MAY 25, 1940

There is no news to indicate that the Allied position is any better and the situation remains very grave and very confused, but there is no reason to lose confidence, according to authoritative circles in London. The absence of news is explained by the special request of the French High Command that no mention be made of troop movements or places where action is taking place. The position of Boulogne and Calais remains obscure, but two things seem to emerge from the welter of rumors, reports, and communiqués.

The Germans are conducting major operations and so far the Allied counteroffensive has been only local. The *Evening Standard*'s military correspondent points out that the idea of the German mechanized units being engaged in a glorified raid is utter and dangerous nonsense. Abbeville, Amiens, and Boulogne are not an automobile bandit's swag, he says. The position is grave, but one frequently hears the comment, "Even if we lose all Belgium and northern France, we won't lose the war." Many Britishers believe that these islands could be turned into a fortress off the coast of Europe, that it could hold out as long as the Navy is afloat and ships continue to arrive. Increased help from America is hoped for and expected. Some surprise is expressed here at American comment stating that the war may be lost before help can come from your side of the Atlantic. Londoners don't take quite such a pessimistic view of the situation. They hope for American aid as nations on the Continent have hoped for British aid in the past. The American re-armament drive is welcomed by the British press, but some of the reports from home have caused a certain amount of amusement over here.

The other day an English friend of mine, after reading the report that several million American women wanted rifles to defend the country from parachutists, said he'd rather stay here and face Hitler's bombs than go to America. He says a few million women with rifles was the most frightening prospect a man could face.

I believe Britain is about to increase her propaganda effort in the United States, and the attitude, as I've heard it, is this. The Americans think we're making propaganda any-way, so why shouldn't we do a better job of it? The British believe they have a good case and a good cause and you can expect them to tell you more about it in the near future.

Here in London the guards around government buildings have been increased and the War Office announces the for-mation of additional defense units to be made up of boys between the ages of eighteen and nineteen and one half. The twenty-seven-year-olds registered for military service today. Slightly more than 1% claimed exemption as con-scientious objectors.

The dropping of a few bombs on England last night hasn't caused much excitement. Only eight civilians were wounded and there was little damage to property. Most people seem to feel that when the Germans decide to bomb this country in earnest, they won't confine themselves to a few isolated spots. There were air-raid warnings in East Kent again tonight but no details are available, but the Air Ministry announcement, however, speaks of a warning and not of an actual raid.

Last night I overheard a conversation between two workmen playing darts in a pub. It went something like this: "What'll we do with 'im, 'Arry?" "Oh, 'e'll probably escape to Switzerland, George." "Well, they're apt to give 'im up. We're going to 'ang 'im when this is over." Those two men were discussing Hitler's fate at a time when the Germans are at the Channel ports and the flower of the British Army is in grave danger and while efforts are being made to lock the British stable. Such optimism may not be warranted—it may be unwise and it's not universal—but it does exist.

Tonight a signal to the Dutch navy crackled out of the transmitters of the British Admiralty. It welcomed such units of the Dutch fleet as had reached England, praised their losing fight against heavy odds, and stressed the achievement of two Dutch submarines just finished building at Rotterdam. These two new submarines successfully negotiated magnetic mine fields and have now reached British ports. Sir Oswald Mosley and some sixty of his associates are still in jail and it's expected that the roundup of Fascist sympathizers will continue and be intensified.

MAY 29, 1940

The latest official communiqué states that Allied forces are fighting fiercely in an effort to make their way to the

coast. Powerful units of the French navy are assisting, trying to defend the ports and communications and to bring
fresh supplies to Dunkerque and to the troops supplied
through that port. So far as we know, Dunkerque remains in
Allied hands.

Those of you who live in Canada may care to know that
another contingent of Canadian airmen arrived in England
yesterday. They report a quiet and uneventful crossing. The
absence of German submarines in the transatlantic sea lanes
has caused considerable comment and speculation here during recent weeks, but it is only comment and speculation.
Britain has always counted itself lucky in being surrounded
by a great ditch. Last night and today I have been down on
the southeast coast. A few miles separated me from German-
held territory. When Napoleon massed his armies behind
Boulogne, ready to invade England, forts and watchtowers
were built along that section of the coast. The forts are now
useless but the old watchtowers are being used by lookout
men. Binoculars and sound detectors sweep the sky. There
are strange obstructions on the flat, smooth esplanade facing the sea. Busses, old cars, and trucks are parked all over
the place, as though left there by drunken drivers, but when
you look carefully you see there's not a spot where an air-
plane can land without ploughing into an obstruction of
some kind. Upon the cliffs the big summer resort hotels are
empty and silent. Deck chairs still stand on green grass in
front of the bandstand but there are no concerts. For days
and nights residents of the towns have heard the murmur
and stutter of guns and bombs across the Channel, but all
was quiet last night and today. Life went on calmly and almost casually. The children are leaving on Sunday. Many

of the older retired folk are leaving, too, but there was no
sign of panic.

I had tea in a big department store. The place was well
stocked with food and clothes. Business was fair. It seemed
a little strange to see antiparachute men leaning their rifles
against chairs when they sat down to tea but, otherwise,
things were very much as they were a year ago down there.
In the amusement center near the shore the little electric
cars continued to bump each other about. The shooting
gallery, equipped with American .22 rifles, was doing fairly
good business. The local editor told me that people were
getting used to the air-raid sirens, but the chief of the air-
raid-precautions organization complained that too many
people called him up after midnight; they disturbed his
sleep. He didn't see why orders and instructions couldn't
be dealt with during the day. It was all right to wake a man
up if the Germans actually came over, but, otherwise, sleep
was important and he didn't think it should be disturbed.

The Germans have claimed that not even a rat can pass
through the Straits of Dover now that Boulogne is in their
hands. Well, I didn't see any rats, but I did see a considerable number of ships going up and down—cargo ships—well
off the English coast. Of course, all that may change when
the Germans have established their heavy guns on the other
side of the ditch. But, as one sailor pointed out to me, it's
easy to hit a town, but a ship three hundred feet long and
fifty feet wide, a ship that is moving, is not such an easy
target. That remains to be seen. But I can tell you that
shipping was passing through the Channel with ease this
afternoon.

Coming back from the coast, we were mixed up with

troop trains, bringing men home on leave. The white dust of France was still on their shoes. Their uniforms were dirty and worn. The men were brown and looked fit and tough. If they were discouraged or defeated, they didn't show it. Most of them were smiling and waving. Only occasionally did you see one who sat staring without seeing, as though trying to remember something he had seen or perhaps trying to forget something he had seen. And that's all from London at 3:40 in the morning.

MAY 30, 1940

The battle around Dunkerque is still raging. The city itself is held by marines and covered by naval guns. The British Expeditionary Force has continued to fall back toward the coast and part of it, including wounded and those not immediately engaged, has been evacuated by sea. Certain units, the strength of which is naturally not stated, are back in England.

The War Office tonight paid its tribute to the small British force that held Calais for several days. By refusing to surrender, the British troops pinned down considerable German forces, enabling British troops farther north to effect their withdrawal on Dunkerque. The War Office statement gives no information concerning that British force at Calais but remarks that its action wrote one of the most brilliant pages in the annals of the British Army. The statement is being repeated here by both press and radio that the British Expeditionary Force's main bases and supply depots were not at the Channel ports. It is admitted that much material has been lost but the main bases have not been taken.

In yesterday's air action, seventy-seven German planes were brought down with the loss of only ten British aircraft, according to an Air Ministry statement.

On the home front, new defense measures are being announced almost hourly. Any newspaper opposing the prosecution of the war can now be suppressed. Neutral vessels arriving in British ports are being carefully searched for concealed troops. Refugees arriving from the Continent are being closely questioned in an effort to weed out spies. More restrictions on home consumption and increased taxation are expected. Signposts are being taken down on the roads that might be used by German forces invading this country. Upon hearing about the signposts, an English friend of mine remarked, "That's going to make a fine shumuzzle. The Germans drive on the right and we drive on the left. There'll be a jolly old mixup on the roads if the Germans do come."

One of the afternoon papers finds space to print a cartoon showing an elderly aristocratic Englishman, dressed in his antiparachute uniform, saying to his servant, who holds a double-barrel shotgun, "Come along, Thompson. I shall want you to load for me." The Londoners are doing their best to preserve their sense of humor, but I saw more grave, solemn faces today than I have ever seen in London. Fashionable tearooms were almost deserted; the shops in Bond Street were doing very little business; people read their newspapers as they walked slowly along the streets. Even the newsreel theaters were nearly empty. I saw one woman standing in line waiting for a bus begin to cry, very quietly.

She didn't even bother to wipe the tears away. In Regent Street there was a sandwich man—his sign in big red letters had only three words on it: WATCH AND PRAY.

Those Englishmen who maintain doubts concerning the imminence of the German threat to this country probably lost these doubts tonight as a result of a broadcast by Malcolm MacDonald, the Minister of Health. Mr. MacDonald said flatly that the government considered the risk of early bombing so real that they had decided to ask all parents in danger areas to register their children for evacuation. Children will leave the coast towns, that is, on the south and southeast coasts, on Sunday, and Mr. MacDonald warned that it might be necessary to evacuate other areas next week.

MAY 31, 1940

We are told tonight that the Allied forces are holding out around Dunkerque and that bad weather has decreased German air activities. The evacuation of Allied troops from the area around Dunkerque continues. Barges, lifeboats, paddle steamers, anything that will float, are being used to take them off. This evacuation is being carried out from open beaches. No figures can be given concerning the total number saved, but there is reason to believe that more men will be taken off than appeared possible two days ago.

Here beside me is a British soldier, a private. He drove the first British car that rolled across the frontier into Belgium. Since then he's done a great deal of traveling and some fighting, but that's his story and here he is to tell it.

The Soldier: "We were retreating with the remnants of the Belgian division, which had seen very heavy fighting the previous day. We had been bombed and machine-gunned from the air continuously since dawn. As many as thirty or forty planes were over us at the time. About six o'clock in the evening we were being bombed by sixteen Dorniers when suddenly four Spitfires appeared. The first ones we had seen. Within six minutes they had brought down four Dorniers, the others broke and dispersed. Further Dorniers fell within a few yards of our column. The pilots and crew were burned, but one of the machine guns was intact. One of our fellows dismantled the German machine gun and got around seven hundred rounds of ammunition in drums. He mounted it on a sidecar. Two days later we were bombed at dawn by a Heinkel. One of our troopers rushed over to the sidecar and set the Heinkel down with that German machine gun. Everybody was firing at the German plane but I think it was the German gun that brought it down. We got another seven hundred and sixty rounds of ammunition out of that one and we used that to knock them out. The enemy have been bombing the bayside all day trying to get that small boat. Just at dusk he shot down one of their Heinkels and then swept low over the stretch we were sheltering. We gave him a burst of machine-gun fire and brought him down. The motorcycles were sent out to pick him up as he parachuted down and he is now safe in England. Coming over in our little ship, I was walking around what we call the sharp end of the ship when I heard a swishing noise. I half turned and saw a motor torpedo boat about twenty yards away. It let go the first torpedo and then another one, but they both missed. I fired my rifle when I realized it wasn't one of ours and the second mate rushed out shouting about it. The captain came running with a gun and we kept on firing away as fast as we could at the Germans. When he realized he hadn't sunk us he came around again and ordered us to stop, but we didn't stop. He then circled at a wider distance. Actually in this spot he was about thirty-five or forty yards away, running around us. As he went around we crossed oversides and kept rattling bullets at him as fast as we could. There was a fellow, Mogree, an Irishman, and this fellow hadn't a rifle. He had a revolver but on this occasion he got hold of a rifle which I loaded and he emptied the magazine and then very politely asked me would I mind loading it again, please, so that he could have another go.

"The fight lasted something like twenty minutes. The Germans were using machine guns. We could see the tracer marks flying over the deck like fireworks. He got some of us but he wasn't much good. We finally silenced him and when he finally drifted across our stern he was only five or six yards away and there was no sign of life at all. First we thought of towing him, but we wanted to get away as quickly as we could, so we just left him there. We were lucky to get him because, if we hadn't, he would have prob-ably fetched his pals and had another go. That's how we got back to England."

That was a British pilot, the first man who crossed with the British Expeditionary Force into Belgium and who reached England recently.

JUNE 1, 1940

The evacuation of British and French troops in the area around Dunkerque has continued throughout the day. It is stated here that the withdrawal is proceeding satisfactorily.

Lord Gort, Commander in Chief of the British field forces, arrived in London this morning. He was met by Mr. Eden, the Secretary of State for War. Lord Gort then had a series of conferences at the War Office. Later today he was received by the King, who made him a Knight Grand Cross of the Order of the Bath. That award, one of the highest in this country, is significant. It means that the government has officially put the stamp of approval upon Lord Gort's conduct of the Flanders campaign.

During the day I've driven one hundred and fifty miles in southern and southeast England. Most of that part of the country is soft, green, and rolling, interlaced with winding, hard-surfaced roads. The road signs are all gone; signs giving the names of towns and villages have been removed. Working parties of soldiers are putting up barricades; gun emplacements are being prepared at strategic crossroads. Driving along through hop fields or between high hedges, I often noticed old trucks, tractors, and farm carts parked in the bushes, ready to be pushed out into the road. A dozen times I was stopped by sentries with fixed bayonets, who asked very politely to see my credentials. It was like crossing the frontiers of a dozen states on the Continent in peacetime. The complete absence of road signs and place names is confusing. The only thing to tell the traveler that Canterbury is Canterbury is the big cathedral rising out of the plain. There are no signs—there are no signs pointing to London, Cambridge, Wells, Seven Oaks, or anywhere else.

I know that part of the country fairly well, and coming up to London tonight I wished for a compass. Occasionally a squad of big British bombers, possibly coming back from

Dunkerque, growled overhead. At other times sleek, fast fighters whined away toward the coast in search of German bombers, probably to be found not more than ten minutes' flying distance away. Occasionally, at towns and villages on the railroad leading up from the south coast, crowds of people gathered around the railway station, watching ambulances pick up their loads from the troop trains.

The war hasn't really arrived down in that corner of England, but it's much nearer than would have seemed possible a month ago. Part of this afternoon I spent at an airfield, talking with pilots who had just stepped out of their planes after coming back from Dunkerque. I hope to be able to tell you something about those boys tomorrow night.

JUNE 2, 1940—8 A.M.

We are told today that most of the British Expeditionary Force is home from Flanders. There are no official figures of the number saved, but the unofficial estimates claim that as much as two thirds or perhaps four fifths of the force has been saved. It is claimed here that not more than one British division remains in the Dunkerque area. It may be that these estimates are unduly optimistic, but it's certainly true that a week ago few people believed that the evacuation could have been carried out so successfully.

There is a tendency on the part of some writers in the Sunday press to call the withdrawal a victory, and there will be disagreement on that point. But the least that can be said is that the Navy, Army and Air Force gilded defeat with glory. Military experts here agree that the operation has been the most successful in British military history. The

withdrawal from Gallipoli during the last war does not com-
pare with the removal of these troops from the pocket in
northern France. The Gallipoli withdrawal was done in
secrecy. There was no threat of air attacks. The action was
spread over twenty-one nights. One hundred and twenty
thousand men were removed at that time. During this operation it is reliably reported that a considerably larger number
was taken off in five days under incessant bombing and during the last two days under long-range German artillery fire.

The Navy is pleased with its share in the operation and
sees substantiation for its claim that the German fleet was
badly mauled in the Norwegian campaign. They see confirmation of this in the fact that the German navy did not
attempt serious interference during the withdrawal. Naval
experts here say that the sea action offered an ideal opportunity for the use of German submarines, but there has
been no mention of U-boat action in official or unofficial
reports.

The German air arm was apparently entrusted with the
job of stopping the British withdrawal. Goering's fliers had
plenty of planes and no lack of targets. But according to the
British view, they were unable to interfere seriously with
seagoing movement.

London reports claim that German losses in Flanders
were far in excess of those suffered by the Allies. It's also
claimed that the material destruction inflicted upon the
Germans, particularly their air force, is much greater than
anything suffered by British naval units in the course of
their action.

About five years ago the Committee of Imperial Defense
here in London estimated that forty-three aircraft repre-

sented the cash value of one battleship. On the basis of these figures, the German air losses last week represent the equivalent of about five big battleships. Against that must be placed the British-announced loss of three destroyers, one small transport, and several small auxiliary craft. The conclusion drawn from all this is that sea power is still of vital importance, that air bombing has not removed sea power from its foremost place in strategy, and that's an important conclusion for the British at a time when Berlin is breathing threats of an invasion of this country.

The main subject of speculation here today is what will Hitler do next? He still has the initiative and a choice of several alternatives. He may hold the line of the Somme and the Aisne and launch his attack against this country. He may re-form his tank divisions and attempt to smash through to Paris, perhaps with his good friend Mussolini hitting the French in the south. He may do both of these things simultaneously or he may offer peace terms to Paris. The best opinion here seems to be that he will not attempt two operations at once, since the whole history of German strategy seems to prove that he will concentrate upon a single objective. His strength so far has lain in the co-operation of his mechanized units and his air force. The Somme-Aisne line, now held by the Allies, is longer and less well defended than the line on the Belgian frontier through which he smashed three weeks ago.

As a result of these considerations, the weight of the guessing here today is that a supreme effort will be made to knock France out of the war during the next few weeks.

There is no disposition here to conceal the fact that the British Expeditionary Force was inadequately equipped with armor and with guns, and above everything else they didn't have sufficient aircraft. The responsibility for this state of affairs rests squarely upon the men who led this country until a few weeks ago. They purchased a few months of normal living and normal working, while assuring the country that all was well and that time was on the side of the Allies. But they bought that quiet and complacency in an expensive market. There is no indication, however, that the British are wanting to hold a post-mortem at this time. Many of the men who directed the affairs of this country until recently are still in high office, but very little is heard of them. The only mention of Mr. Neville Chamberlain to appear in the press during the last ten days is in the form of a speculation or prophecy that he will shortly retire from public life, or be created a peer of the realm and sent to the House of Lords, which means pretty well the same thing.

Several times in the course of the last few weeks I've told you something of the German radio propaganda aimed at this country. You might be interested to hear one or two examples of what London is telling Germany by way of the radio. The other night a German-speaking announcer in London told the Germans about hospital trains that go through Germany close together and said that when they passed through a town or village, the air-raid siren is sounded so that people go underground and don't see those long trains of wounded soldiers passing through German cities and villages.

JUNE 2, 1940—7 P.M.

Yesterday I spent several hours at what may be tonight or

next week Britain's first line of defense, an airfield on the southeast coast. The German bases weren't more than ten minutes' flying time away—across that ditch that has protected Britain and conditioned the thinking of Britishers for centuries. I talked with pilots as they came back from Dunkerque. They stripped off their light jackets, glanced at a few bulletholes in wings or fuselage, and as their ground crews swarmed over the aircraft, refueling motors and guns, we sat on the ground and talked. Out in the middle of the field the wreckage of a plane was being cleared up. It had crashed the night before. The pilot had been shot in the head, but managed to get back to his field. The Royal Air Force prides itself on never walking out of a plane until it falls apart.

I can tell you what those boys told me. They were the cream of the youth of Britain. As we sat there, they were waiting to take off again. They talked of their own work, discussed the German air force with all the casualness of Sunday-morning quarterbacks discussing yesterday's football game. There were no nerves, no profanity, and no heroics. There was no swagger about those boys in wrinkled and stained uniforms. The movies do that sort of thing much more dramatically than it is in real life.

They told me of the patrol from which they'd just returned. "Six Germans downed. We lost two." "What happened to Eric?" said one. "Oh, I saw him come down right alongside one of our destroyers," replied another. "The Germans fight well in a crowd. They know how to use the sun, and if they surprise you, it's uncomfortable. If twenty or so of them catch five of us, we stay and fight," they said. "Maybe that's why we get so many of them," added one boy, with a grin.

They all told the same story about numbers. "Six of us go over," they said, "and we meet twelve Germans." "If ten of us go, there's twenty Germans." But they were all anxious to go again.

When the squadron took off, one of them remarked quite casually that he'd be back in time for tea. About that time a boy of twenty drove up in a station wagon. He weighed about one hundred and fifteen pounds. He asked the squadron leader if he could have someone to fly him back to his own field. His voice was loud and flat; his uniform was torn, had obviously been wet. He wore a pair of brown tennis shoes, three sizes too big. After he'd gone I asked one of the men who had been talking with him what was the matter with him. "Oh," he replied, "he was shot down over at Dunkerque, on the first patrol this morning. Landed in the sea, swam to the beach, was bombed for a couple of hours, came home in a paddle steamer. His voice sounds like that because he can't hear himself. You get that way after you've been bombed a few hours," he said.

JUNE 4, 1940

I sat in the House of Commons this afternoon and heard Winston Churchill, Britain's tired old man of the sea, sum up the recent operations. He tried again, as he has tried for nearly ten years, to warn this country of the threat that impends. He told of the 335,000 troops, British and French, brought back from Dunkerque. British losses exceed 30,000—

killed, wounded, and missing. Enormous material losses were sustained. He described how the eight or nine German armored divisions swept like a sharp scythe to the right and rear of the northern armies. But the thrust did not reach Dunkerque, because of the resistance put up at Boulogne and Calais. Only thirty unwounded survivors were taken off from the port of Calais. A grave situation was made worse by the capitulation of the King of the Belgians, a pitiful episode, said Mr. Churchill.

He then paid his tribute to the Royal Air Force. It decisively defeated the main strength of the German air force, inflicting losses of at least four to one. As he talked of those young fliers, greater than knights of the round table, crusaders of old, Mr. Churchill needed only wings and an engine to take off. But wars, he said, are not won by evacuations. Nearly a thousand guns had been lost. All transport and all armored vehicles with the northern armies had been lost. A colossal military disaster had occurred, and another blow must be expected almost immediately. Home defense must be built up. And there will be a secret session on that subject next week.

Mr. Churchill believed that these islands could be successfully defended, could ride out the storm of war and outlive the menace of tyranny . . . if necessary for years . . . if necessary, alone.

There was a prophetic quality about that speech. We shall go on to the end, he said; we shall fight in France, we shall fight on the seas and oceans, we shall fight on the beaches, in the fields, in the streets, in the hills; we shall never surrender. If this island or a large part of it were subjugated and starving, then the Empire beyond the seas, armed and guarded by the British fleet, would carry on the struggle until, in God's good time, the New World with all its power and might sets forth to the rescue and liberation of the Old.

With those words, the Prime Minister sat down. I have heard Mr. Churchill in the House of Commons at intervals over the last ten years. I heard his speech on the Norwegian campaign, and I have some knowledge of his writings. To-day, he was different. There was little oratory; he wasn't interested in being a showman. He spoke the language of Shakespeare with a direct urgency such as I have never before heard in that House. There were no frills and no tricks. Winston Churchill's speeches have been prophetic. He has talked and written of the German danger for years. He has gone into the political wilderness in defense of his ideas. Today, as Prime Minister, he gave the House of Commons a report remarkable for its honesty, inspiration, and gravity.

The evacuation of Dunkerque, according to Paris reports, has been completed. No more men will be taken off from those bloodstained beaches. There was little air activity in that area yesterday. The Royal Air Force has continued its efforts to destroy fuel tanks captured by the Germans in Belgium and Holland. Reconnaissance aircraft has been busy on both sides. There is a breathing space tonight, but no one here expects it to last long.

V

June 17 to September 2, 1940

JUNE 17, 1940. *The French government rejects a British proposal for Franco-British Union and appeals to Germany for an honorable end to hostilities.*

JUNE 22. *French delegation signs armistice terms with Germans at Compiègne.*

JUNE 24. *After two weeks of war, the French sign a separate armistice with Italy.*

JUNE 27. *Rumania agrees to cede Russian Bessarabia and Northern Bukovina to the Soviet Union and permits Soviet naval forces to have access to Black Sea ports.*

JULY 2. *The new French government establishes headquarters at Vichy.*

JULY 3. *British warships destroy part of French fleet in North African naval base of Oran.*

JULY 4. *Rumania establishes a pro-German anti-Semitic Cabinet.*

JULY 25. *The Pétain government breaks off relations with Britain as result of the battle of Oran.*

JULY 10. *French Parliament at Vichy votes Pétain dictatorial powers.*

AUGUST 12. *Russia abandons the political commissar system in the Red Army whereby Communist functionaries had equal power with military commanders except in actual combat.*

AUGUST 15. *After several weeks of increased air activity over Britain, the Germans send wave after wave of war planes over Scotland and England.*

AUGUST 19. *British abandon Somaliland to the Italians.*

AUGUST 22. German planes launch first mass night attack on London.

AUGUST 25. British planes raid Berlin.

AUGUST 27. Attorney General Jackson informs President Roosevelt that Constitution does not require consent of Congress to exchange fifty over-age destroyers for right of United States to use British naval and air bases in the Western Hemisphere. The President therefore concluded the deal and informed the public on September 3.

AUGUST 30. German and Italian Foreign Ministers acting as arbiters grant Hungary about half the Rumanian province of Transylvania.

SEPTEMBER 2. Germans send 700 planes against Britain in three attempts to destroy London. British deaths from German air raids in August averaged slightly less than thirty-five per day.

BRITAIN STANDS ALONE

JUNE 17, 1940

A few minutes ago, a spokesman of the British Foreign Office stated that the French decision to cease hostilities would not in any way affect the British determination to carry on the war alone and to the end.

You will want to know how the British took last night's announcement of the creation of a new French government. In the first place, there was no official announcement until a few minutes ago. There have been no recriminations against the French. On the surface London is calm. Few people would have been surprised last night to learn that the French armies had laid down their arms. If the French conclude a peace and if their navy should be taken over or immobilized, the shock would be the greatest this country has ever sustained. But you will find difficulty in locating an Englishman who would talk seriously of the possibility of peace with Germany now. The British were warned by Churchill two weeks ago that they might have to fight alone, that there would be fighting on the beaches, the landing grounds, in the hills and the streets. That prophecy is near to being fulfilled.

No one can presume to speak for a nation on a day like this. But I believe that the people of this country realize the difference between this war and previous wars. In the old days, a war could be lost—a few colonies or provinces ceded to the enemy—and the vanquished could then begin to prepare for the next time. These people are pretty well convinced there won't be any next time if this war is lost.

This afternoon's *Evening Standard* says the task of this nation is clear and simple. It is to transform this country into a single fortress. The sea, it says, is still our strength. This island which floats upon it must become a vast battleship, thickly armored and hugely gunned. If the last fortress holds, mankind is saved. In general, the afternoon press is telling the people of this country that in a few days or weeks they will be fighting for their homes. The demand that children and surplus civilians be moved out of danger areas is renewed, and there are pictures of civilians drilling with broomsticks, because there aren't enough rifles to go around.

The Russians are creeping down the Baltic, but few Britishers have time to think of the extinction of those three small states created by British and French arms at the end of the last war. The opinion is that the Russians, disconcerted by the German success, are doing a little more grabbing while they have the opportunity. But even the most hopeful do not predict that the Russians will attack Germany.

Many people here are wondering what the effect will be upon American opinion and policy when the French are forced out of the war. Two newspapers at opposite ends of the political spectrum offer editorial advice to America today. The big, conservative *Daily Express* says: "America should learn by our own experience. Her citizens have reached the stage that we in Europe were at the time of

Munich, when we were racked with anxiety. Afterwards, we breathed a sigh of relief and sank gently into a complacency that now astounds and humiliates us. Now we are suffering the most stupendous reverses. America," says the *Daily Express*, "don't be English. Don't accept the soft words of reassurance that come from Germany; there is no time for subtlety now. We give you advice from the bitterness of our own lessons."

The Labour party's *Daily Herald* wants the American people to decide with their eyes open and not make the same tragic mistakes as Hitler's other threatened victims, of hoping that whomever else he struck, he would somehow leave them alone. The *Herald* concludes: "For Americans' own sake, we fervently trust that they too will not be lulled until almost too late by the wishful nightmare of appeasement and the slogans of splendid isolation."

JUNE 19, 1940

The British are naturally interested in the outcome of the negotiations between France and the Axis, but attention is centered mainly on the Battle for Britain. It is hoped that something can be saved of the French forces in overseas positions, but the main drive here is behind preparations for the defense of these islands. This morning the mailman delivered millions of little circulars to British homes. I have one of them here. At first glance it looks like one of those circulars advertising bargain day at the local grocery store at home. But this little circular is headed *"If The Invader Comes."* It contains six rules or directions. The first is: "Remain where you are." The second: "Don't believe rumors and don't spread them. When you receive an order, be sure that it is official and not faked." Three: "Keep watch; if you see anything suspicious, make your report to the authorities brief and factual." Four: "Don't give any German anything; don't tell him anything; hide your food, bicycles, and maps; see that he gets no gasoline." Five: "Be ready to help the military in any way, but don't go blocking roads or streets until you are told to do so." And sixth: "All factories and shops must organize some system by which a sudden attack can be resisted. Think always of your country before you think of yourself" is the final piece of advice.

The House of Commons will be told this afternoon details of a scheme to send 200,000 children overseas to the Dominions and perhaps to the United States. Parents will not be able to go with their children, but it is expected that they will have to contribute to the cost of transportation. The fare to Canada for children over fourteen is about $150. No one knows how many parents will be willing to let their children go, but steamship and passport offices have been jammed for the last two days with mothers attempting to make arrangements to send their children out of the country. Probably not many poor people will be able or willing to send their children. There is still something like 345,000 children in London, children whose parents have refused to send them to safer areas.

People who have been working on the evacuation of London children tell me that poor people often say their children are all they've got and they won't part with them. If they refuse to send them to the country, they certainly won't send them overseas. Then, too, there's always the thought of the transports being torpedoed. That's why a lot of people over here are hoping that some of those American ships with the stars and stripes floodlit on their decks and sides will be sent over to take some of the children off. There are going to be an awful lot of hungry children in Europe next winter and not all of them will be in England.

JULY 14, 1940

"We await undismayed the impending assault. Perhaps it will come tonight, perhaps it will come next week, perhaps it will never come. We must show ourselves equally capable of meeting a sudden violent shock or what is perhaps a harder task, a prolonged vigil. But be the ordeal sharp or long, or both, we shall seek no terms, we shall tolerate no parley, we may show mercy—we ask none." In those words Prime Minister Winston Churchill summed up the position of Britain tonight, and his listeners in British homes everywhere, in public houses, in barracks, and on the high seas know that so long as he's leader of this country, those words represent for them completely the fears and hopes of this Empire.

The war, according to Mr. Churchill, will be long and hard. The invasion of Britain today will be an entirely different proposition to what it was two months ago. Never before has Britain had in this island an army comparable in quantity, equipment, or numbers to that which stands on guard here tonight. Britain has, said Mr. Churchill, larger food reserves than she has ever had and a substantially larger tonnage under her own flag, apart from hundreds of foreign ships, than she had at the beginning of the war. Warning against any slackening of efforts or vigilance, the Prime

Minister said, "We must prepare not only for the summer, but for the winter. Not only for 1941, but for 1942 when the war will, I trust, take a different form from the defensive in which it has hitherto been bound."

Last night fourteen airdomes in Holland and Germany were bombed, and the British suffered no loss.

The final score of yesterday's German attacks on shipping and coastal towns is given as twelve German planes downed, three British fighters lost. This afternoon a British convoy was passing through the Straits of Dover, close in shore. German dive bombers came out to the attack. A radio recording van was standing on the cliffs above Dover and to-night British listeners heard an eyewitness account of the biggest air battle of the day. They heard the cough of anti-aircraft fire and the stutter of machine guns overhead. Heard the commentator with only the faintest trace of excitement in his voice describe a German pilot bailing out of his smoking machine. There was a pause while the commentator waited for the parachute to open. Roaring out of the loud-speakers of Britain tonight came the thunder of one-thousand-horsepower motors of British fighters as they swept out over the Channel in two flights—the first to engage the German fighter escort and the second to tackle the bombers. Later we heard a description of Spitfires and Hurricanes driving Messerschmitts back toward the French coast.

JULY 21, 1940

Occasionally, in reporting this war, the reporter is obliged to express his personal opinion, his own evaluation of the mass of confusing and contradictory statements, communiqués, speeches by statesmen, and personal interviews. It has always seemed to me that such statements of personal opinion should be frankly labeled as such without any attempt to cloak one's own impressions or opinions in an aura of omnipotence. What I think of events in Europe is no more important than what you think, but I do have certain opportunities for observation and study. The result of that observation and study leads me to believe that Britain faces four—or rather, five—immediate tasks. The first is to repel invasion when and if it comes. The second, to make the blockade of the Continent as effective as possible. Third, to devise measures for defeating the Axis blockade of these islands; and fourth, to prepare to take the offensive. But the fifth task is of equal if not greater importance. The necessary unity, determination, fervor, and, if you will, fanaticism must be developed and maintained in this country to permit the carrying out of the first four items. An increasing number of people appear to be realizing that Britain will never again return to the conditions that prevailed the day before war was declared.

During the last war many things, from the emancipation of women to the adoption of summer time, occurred in this country, things which in peacetime would have been called revolutionary. Those things have remained. There have been and will be other and perhaps more sweeping changes in this war. Frequently these days one hears that quotation from Pitt: "England will save herself by her exertions, and Europe by her example." The exertions in the field of military preparations are unparalleled. The example of the way of life to be held out to the peoples of Europe as an inducement for them to revolt is slowly taking shape under the pressure of wartime demands. If the British succeed in defending these islands against the first German onslaught, if it comes, and against the boredom and desire for even temporary security which will certainly come, then the results of this war may well be determined by the ability of the British to organize the production and the equitable distribution of the resources available to the community.

J. B. Priestley summed up this domestic struggle tonight when he said in a broadcast that it was a contest between power and property, on the one hand, and the community and creativeness, on the other. He told of a big garden lying fallow because its owner had gone to America, while workingmen in the community who hadn't gone to America needed land on which to grow vegetables. Under the existing property concept they couldn't use that idle garden, but a proper regard for community interests would certainly demand that the garden be used. This ferment of change is called by some a revolution by consent, a revolt against too-long rule by old men whose ideal for their country was a comfortable old age. It is an attempt by Britain to hammer out in the host of war a workable answer to the totalitarian concept, an attempt to achieve social justice without smashing the unity of the nation or unduly restricting the liberty of the individual. It is a result of the realization that the hopeless and bewildered on the Continent of Europe who have turned to dictatorship must be offered an example and an alternative more attractive and more workable than that presented by European democracies of the last twenty years. It is basically Britain's effort to recapture the moral leadership of Europe. The success or failure of the effort depends in the first instance on the result of the trial at arms that impends.

AUGUST 4, 1940

This is August bank holiday in England, but it's a holiday in name only. Traditionally, everything in Britain closes down for four days over this week end and everyone who can goes to the seaside. The coast to Britain then resembled one vast Coney Island, but this year there is no holiday, and the coasts are deserted except for those soldiers, sailors, and airmen who are preparing to fight unwelcome visitors from across the North Sea and the Channel. I spent the last three days at a Channel port. It was a rather dull three days. Radio and press correspondents sat around the leading hotel, waiting for the air-raid siren. The food was good, plentiful, and cheap. In the evening the lounge was crowded with Navy, Army, and Air Force officers. The Army still favors the close-clipped mustache, black brier pipe, wrist watch on the left wrist, and identity disk attached by a silver chain to the right wrist. Pink gin remains the favorite drink of the Navy, but the Army and Air Force give preference to beer or Scotch and soda. Just across the way from the hotel there was a roller-skating rink where sailors and soldiers off duty might skate or fall down to the tune of *Annie Doesn't Live Here Any More* or *The Man Who Broke the Bank at Monte Carlo*. The local goldsmith displayed a neatly lettered little sign informing his customers that he would take good care of their watches and jewelry left for repair but couldn't be responsible for losses due to enemy action.

The town's leading bootmaker had enough prewar leather

on hand to last for two years and was busy making shoes and boots for people he had seen, from lasts made by his father forty years ago. He didn't seem the least bit worried by the fact that the Germans were only a few miles away. When the air-raid siren sounded we jumped into our cars and drove up to the cliffs overlooking the town and the Channel. The white cliffs and the green fields of France were clearly visible on the other side. It almost seemed that we should be able to see the German planes taking off. A screen of British fighters came roaring out over the Channel and swept down in front of us and then back again. The antiaircraft gunners stripped the canvas jackets from their guns and the observers wearing headphones swung their big sound detectors. But it soon became clear that the action was away to our left, out of sight. Sometimes when the Germans come over above the clouds it is possible to hear the whisper of high-flying aircraft and the growl of fighters diving with full throttle, interspersed with the bursts of machine-gun fire. But nothing can be seen.

These unseen air battles and the air-raid warnings cause no excitement in the town, and five minutes after the all-clear is sounded life goes on as usual. Driving back from those three uneventful days on the coast we passed through the usual number of barricades and road blocks, much strengthened and improved since I last traveled that road a month ago. The towns and villages through which we passed were jammed and crowded with the usual Saturday-evening visitors and shoppers. The roads on the Saturday evening of this August bank holiday were practically deserted. Occasionally one saw children playing about in the sandbank barricades covering bridges and crossroads. People who live down in that county of Kent, one of the most beautiful counties in England, tell me there isn't much talk of the war down there. Most of the talk is about this year's hop harvest, the heavy oat crop, the need for preserving fruit and vegetables for the winter—the sort of thing about which people who live and work on the land always talk.

Driving back to London in these days when there are no road signs and villages and towns have no names is an interesting experience. London's balloon barrage is a valuable landmark. Miles away one can see those balloons against the evening sky, looking like flyspecks on a dirty windowpane. You just drive toward the balloons and finally you are in London.

AUGUST 10, 1940

In the days of peace Britain had a number of distressed areas, regions that had been stripped by mining and industry and left as barren deserts where there was no work. Today distressed areas are being created all around the coast, particularly in those areas where German invasion threatens. People have left their homes, their shops and offices and come inland. Shopkeepers have seen their customers depart, their businesses dwindle, but still they must pay rent and taxes. The government is being urged to provide some measure of relief for these new distressed areas, in order that the nation as a whole may share the sacrifices imposed upon those who live and work, or rather who did live and work in the coastal areas. It's a problem which will tax the resources and the ingenuity of the government seriously during coming months.

There is another problem which the winter will bring if there is no invasion and that is how the morale and spirit of some twenty divisions of troops, many of them from overseas, is to be maintained during the wet, black winter of inactivity. We're assured by responsible officials that Britain will not go hungry during the winter, but it takes more than food to fight a war. Britain's immediate need is for munitions and machines, man power in the factories rather than in the Army. Mr. Bevin, the Minister of Labor, is now undertaking a survey which many people have urged for months. He is conducting an inquiry into the working history of more than a million men. Every man who has been an engineer or a metal worker since 1929 must register and give the details of his experience. Failure to register may involve a fine of four hundred dollars or three months in jail. The Minister of Labor wants to put all the men who have had experience as engineers or metal workers back to work at their old trades and he has the power to tell them where they will work and for what wage.

AUGUST 16, 1940

During the last three days, I have driven more than five hundred miles in the south of England. Many times the sirens sounded and a few times we saw the bombs fall. There is something unreal about this air war over Britain. Much of it you can't see, but the aircraft are up in the clouds, out of sight. Even when the Germans come down to dive-bomb an airfield it's all over in an incredibly short time. You just see a bomber slanting down toward his target; three or four little things that look like marbles fall out, and it seems to take a long time for those bombs to hit the ground. The other day we drove for twenty-five miles through rural country while an air-raid alarm was on. Coasting down the smooth white road between tall green hedges, we would slide through a little village tucked away at the bottom of a hill beside a stream. There would be one gray-stone church, an arched bridge over the stream, perhaps a couple of dozen little brick cottages with red-tiled roofs, and a public house, generally the Farmers' Arms, the Bull & Bush, or something of the kind. That village would be dead, the streets as empty and silent as they were at two in the morning in peacetime. Even the air was quiet and heavy as it is just before a thunderstorm, but standing on the bridge near the church or at the crossroads would be one small middle-aged man, generally with a mustache, generally smoking a pipe, and always wearing a tin hat. He was the air-raid warden in complete command of the village until the "all-clear" sounded—the sole protection against the German bombers, except for the boys in Hurricanes and Spitfires high overhead and the men manning the antiaircraft batteries. In some of the cities and larger towns people stand about in the streets, but the small villages take cover.

Yesterday afternoon I stood at a hotel window and watched the Germans bomb the naval base at Portland, two or three miles away. In the morning I had been through that naval base and dockyard and satisfied myself that the Admiralty communiqués reporting earlier bombings had been accurate. The naval officers, including the admiral, had been kind and courteous, but as I stood and watched huge columns of smoke and fire leap into the air I thought some of those officers and men would no longer be of this world.

As soon as the "all-clear" sounded we jumped into the car and drove to the naval dockyard again. The workers who had been underground were just leaving. We secured permission to go into the dockyard for the second time that day and for the second time talked with the admiral. We asked him for evidence. He said: "Look around for yourselves. They missed us again." And they had—he was right. As we left, a big sergeant of marines at the gate asked us if we had seen the Germans bailing out. It was, he said, a lovely sight.

From what I could see the people down along the coast had been badly shaken. Many of them don't like the sound of the sirens. It's loud, penetrating, and can't very well be ignored. The sirens seem to be about as disturbing and upsetting as the distant crump of bombs. Coming home today we were stopped by a constable in a little village. The street was lined with children and civilians. I pulled over to the side of the road beside a horse-drawn fireman's cart. We didn't know what was happening, thought maybe bombs had fallen. Suddenly from behind us we heard a police car with a loudspeaker: "Clear the street for His Majesty, the King. Hold that horse's head." The police car was followed by a big maroon car carrying the King and a couple of staff officers. Behind that another car and a lone policeman riding a motorcycle. That was all. The local constable waved us ahead and for fifty miles I drove a little ten-horsepowered car just behind the policeman who was just behind the King. We made good time. There was a policeman at each crossroad to keep the main road clear. I saw those country folk as the King saw them and he must have been encouraged. They were a calm-looking, smiling lot of people and most of them know the hum of German planes overhead and the sound of exploding bombs. As I followed that small royal cavalcade over the rolling country (I gained on them going downhill), I wondered in what other country in this mad world can a King, a dictator, or a head of state travel with as little protection. The policeman on the motorcycle didn't even have a pistol. Just as I reached London this afternoon, the air-raid sirens were sounding again, the people were heading for the shelters in orderly fashion. Only a few of them running. I saw no signs of panic. I did see a woman drive through a red light at about sixty miles an hour but that may have had nothing to do with the excitement or preoccupation created by the sirens. A few minutes after the "all-clear" had sounded people were sitting patiently on little canvas stools on the sidewalk outside Queen's Hall, clearing up for tonight's concert.

I have come to the conclusion that bombs that fall some distance away seem very unreal. Queen's Hall is only about half an hour from Croydon, which in the British vernacular caught a pocket last night, but from the attitude of those people on the sidewalk it might have been hundreds of miles away. One thing I do know—that is, that the bombs that drop close to you are real enough.

AUGUST 18, 1940

I spent five hours this afternoon on the outskirts of London. Bombs fell out there today. From what I saw I am convinced that the Germans were after military objectives. Hours of driving and walking plus the production of innumerable passes failed to secure admission to those military areas. Therefore, you will understand that I am talking now only of the people and the damage done in civilian areas. Bombs behave in the most unpredictable manner. Several fell in the working-class districts, cheap, flimsy houses jammed one against the other. One tenant had constructed a sort of lean-to and in it he had a bathroom. That pitiful little bathroom had been sheared away from the house as though by a giant meat cleaver. Windows had been blown out over a wide area, but the window just above the lean-to was intact. A red sponge was still in the soap dish in the bathtub. There was a long row of houses standing above a road. One of them appeared to have been jabbed with a huge, blunt stick. It was just dust and rubble, a pile about ten feet high, but the houses on either side were still standing. Here the auxiliary fire and demolition services were clearing away the wreckage.

Another bomb had fallen in the pathway but had blown only a small hole. Another hit the fence just outside the church and smashed all the stained-glass windows. Two hours after it happened the rector had sent his assistant around to tell the congregation that evening service would be held as usual.

It is indeed surprising how little damage a bomb will do unless, of course, it scores a direct hit. But I found that one bombed house looks pretty much like another bombed house. It's about the people I'd like to talk, the little people who live in those little houses, who have no uniforms and get no decoration for bravery. Those men whose only uniform was a tin hat were digging unexploded bombs out of the ground this afternoon. There were two women who gossiped across the narrow strip of tired brown grass that separated their two houses. They didn't have to open their kitchen windows in order to converse. The glass had been blown out. There was a little man with a pipe in his mouth who walked up and looked at a bombed house and said, "One fell there and that's all." Those people were calm and courageous. About an hour after the "all-clear" had sounded people were sitting in deck chairs on their lawns, reading the Sunday papers. The girls in light, cheap dresses were strolling along the streets. There was no bravado, no loud voices, only a quiet acceptance of the situation. To me those people were incredibly brave and calm. They are the unknown heroes of this war.

This afternoon I saw a military maneuver that I shall remember for a long time—a company of women dressed in Royal Air Force blue marching in close order. Most of them were girls with blond hair and plenty of make-up. They marched well; right arms thrust forward and snapped smartly down after the fashion of the Guards. They swung through a gate into an airdrome that had been heavily bombed only a few hours before. Some of them were probably frightened, but every head was up. Their ranks were steady and most of them were smiling. They were the clerks, the cooks and waitresses going on duty. I was told that three members of the Women's Auxiliary Air Force were killed in a raid there this morning.

After watching and talking with those people this afternoon I am more than ever convinced that they are made of stern stuff. They can take what is coming. Even the women with two or three children clustered about them were steady and businesslike. A policeman showed me a German machine-gun bullet he had picked up in the street. He said,

"I was certainly frightened. Look at my hand. It's still shaking." But it wasn't shaking and I doubt that it had been.

Now, there is room for many opinions about the diplomatic, economic, and military policy of the British government. This country is still ruled by a class, in spite of Miss Dorothy Thompson's broadcast to this country the other night in which she informed Mr. Churchill that he is the head of a socialist state. If the people who rule Britain are made of the same stuff as the little people I have seen today, if they understand the stuff of which the people who work with their hands are made, and if they trust them, then the defense of Britain will be something of which men will speak with awe and admiration so long as the English language survives. Politicians have repeatedly called this a people's war. These people deserve well of their leaders.

AUGUST 25, 1940

The damage done by an exploding bomb to windows in a given area is a freakish sort of thing. A bomb may explode at an intersection and the blast will travel down two streets, shattering windows for a considerable distance, while big windows within a few yards of the bomb crater remain intact. The glass, incidentally, generally falls out into the street, rather than being blown inwards. During the last two weeks I spent a considerable amount of time wandering about the south and southeast coast in an open car. Much of the time was spent in that section which has been termed by some journalists, but not by the local inhabitants, as Hell's Corner. Now an open car is not to be recommended under normal conditions, for the weather isn't right, but it's helpful these days to be able to look and listen as you drive along. I've seen a number of air battles and bombings and heard more. Perhaps this is a good time to give one observer's impressions, something in the nature of an interim report.

There are no refugees filling the roads leading inland from these coast towns. I saw a double-ended baby carriage containing twins being wheeled along the streets of Dover and rather wished something could be done about that. But the strongest impression one gets of these bombings is a sense of unreality. Often the planes are so high that even in a cloudless sky you can't see them. I stood on a hill watching an airdrome being bombed two miles away. It looked and sounded like farmers blasting stumps in western Washington. You forget entirely that there are men down there on the ground. Even when the dive bombers come down looking like a duck with both wings broken and you hear the hollow grunt of their bombs, it doesn't seem to have much meaning. It's almost impossible to realize that men are killing and being killed, even when you see that ever-thickening streak of smoke pouring down from the sky, which means a plane and perhaps several men going down in flames. On the other hand, when the bombs fall near by, it's possible to assume the most undignified position in the world without effort and without thinking. The position officially recommended: flat on the ground, face down, mouth slightly open, and hands covering ears. Even then the bombs somehow don't seem to make as much noise as they should, but they do seem real. In one village you see people standing in doorways all staring in the same direction, their faces, expressionless, reflect no fear and little anxiety. It's another village or another town that's being bombed. I don't believe the proceedings seem very real to them either.

The other night I heard that screaming bomb come down —the one that fell in the City of London. My own thought was: that one's a safe distance away; there is no need for me to take up the officially recommended position. I'm trying to tell you that this business of being bombed and watching air fights is the sort of thing which fails to produce the anticipated reaction. The sense of danger, death, and disaster comes only when the familiar incidents occur—the things that one has associated with tragedy since childhood. The sight of half a dozen ambulances weighted down with an unseen cargo of human wreckage has jarred me more than the war of dive bombers or the sound of bombs. Another thing that has meaning is fire. Again that's something we can understand.

Last night as I stood on London Bridge with Vincent Sheean and watched that red glow in the sky, it was possible to understand that that's fire as the result of an act of war, but the act itself, even the sound of the bomb that started the fire, was still unreal. What had happened was that three or four high-school boys with some special training had been flying around over London in about $100,000 worth of machinery. One of them had pressed a button— the fire and a number of casualties was the result. We could see the fire and hear the clanging of the fire-engine bells, but we hadn't seen the bomber—had barely heard him. Maybe the children who are now growing up will in future wars be able to associate the sound of bombs, the drone of engines, and the carrying sound of machine guns overhead with human tragedy and disaster. But for me the ambulance and the red flare of fire in the night sky are the outward signs of death and destruction.

AUGUST 26, 1940

This is London at half-past three in the morning. The air raid over the London area is still in progress. The drone of a number of planes can be heard in the sky. A little while ago the searchlight was aimed following the sound of an aircraft which appeared to be making a circular tour of London.

No words of mine can describe the spectacle over London tonight, so I'll talk about the people underground. I visited eleven air-raid shelters in the West End of London during this raid—the longest we've had so far. In one a Scotsman was holding twenty-five people enthralled with the story of the big fish that got away. Over near Wimpole Street two stories underground a man was telling about the narrow escape he had when driving on the icy roads of the Midlands last winter. Two babies looking like well-wrapped dolls slept on a hard wooden bench. At another shelter the warden proclaimed that every time he picked out the sound of a German bomber overhead a blinking car went past overhead and got him all confused.

Each time I entered a new shelter people wanted to know if I'd seen any bombs and was it safe to go home. At one shelter there was a fine row going on. A man wanted to smoke his pipe in the shelter; the warden wouldn't allow it. The pipe smoker said he'd go out and smoke it in the street, where he'd undoubtedly be hit by a bomb and then the warden would be sorry. At places where peat is available, it's being consumed in great quantities at night. I have seen a few pale faces, but very few. How long these people will stand up to this sort of thing I don't know, but tonight they're magnificent. I've seen them, talked with them, and I know.

SEPTEMBER 3, 1940

This is London, three-thirty in the morning. A year ago tonight the weather was warm and muggy. It's the same tonight. Twelve months ago tonight we had a violent thunderstorm. As lightning streaked the sky and thunder rode down these crooked streets, I saw white-faced people running for air-raid shelters. If there should be a similiar storm tonight, there would be no panic: nerves are much steadier, London is not as black tonight as it was on that first night when darkness settled over Europe. Now we have dim little street lights and shaded automobile headlights. Then the theaters and movies were closed. Now they're open and doing good business. London's buildings were splotched with yellow, new sandbags; but the winter rains and summer sun have turned them black. Many have been covered with concrete or boards. Today there are more TO RENT signs in the fashionable residential districts. Those trenches that gashed the green of London parks have been walled up and roofed over to form regular air-raid shelters. Many iron railings around the parks have been taken down. We have sandbags and barbed wires around government buildings. Last year there were many Italian restaurants in Soho, but when Italy entered the war they became Swiss overnight. A year ago we saw only British troops on the street. Now there are Australians, New Zealanders, Canadians, Poles, Czechs, Norwegians, Dutch, Belgians, and French.

The cost of living has gone up. Taxes have gone up. Automobile showrooms have closed. The number of balloons overhead has increased. So has the number of fire engines and ambulances. A few houses on the outskirts of London have been smashed by bombs.

But, in spite of all these changes, the face of London has altered little during the first year of this war. This year, which has brought an unending succession of disaster and disappointment to London, has left few visible signs. The real transformation can only be sensed; it can't be seen. For example, the little brick house in that blind alley known as Downing Street looks just as it did, but there's a new man living at No. 10, and certainly one of the greatest changes of the year occurred when Mr. Chamberlain moved out and Mr. Churchill moved in.

In September, 1939, the talk was of the Navy, the ring of steel that was to starve the Germans. Today the Royal Air Force has captured the respect and admiration which has traditionally been given to the Royal Navy.

On the day war was declared any man who predicted that after a year of war, including only ten weeks of battle, Britain would be without effective allies and faced with the prospect of invasion would have been considered mad. Invasion is now one of the favorite topics of conversation. These Londoners know what they're fighting for now—not Poland or Norway—not even for France, but for Britain.

Men who scoffed at the idea of parachute troops now

spend their nights watching for them. No longer do we hear the sound of church bells on Sunday morning. They will be rung only to announce the arrival of air-borne troops.

There were no seaside holidays for Londoners this year. The beaches are being reserved and prepared for fighting. Newspapers and magazines have been reduced in size. The publication of serious books has decreased. Night clubs are doing a roaring business. The intellectual—the man who can write and talk—now counts for even less than he did a year ago; the man who can run a lathe, fly a plane, or build a ship counts for more.

There is little talk of politics, although the demand that Mr. Chamberlain and some of his colleagues resign continues. London's clubs are carrying on, most of them with reduced membership. But elderly men doze away the afternoon in those big leather chairs just as they have done for years. Occasionally, you hear a retired colonel voice a complaint. He'll say, "We whipped the Boche once in the old uniform, and could have done it again, sir."

The King and Queen are two of the busiest people in these islands. They go about inspecting ships, guns, canteens, factories, and nearly everything else. The King spends considerable time decorating his soldiers, sailors, and airmen.

But one thing has happened to London or, rather, to Londoners which can only be appreciated by one who has spent considerably more than a year in this sprawling city beside the Thames: they've become more human, less reserved; more talkative and less formal. There's almost a small-town atmosphere about the place. Sometimes strangers speak to you in the bus or subways. I've even heard a conversation between total strangers in a railway car—something which was unthinkable in peacetime. There's been a drawing together, particularly during the last two months. Part of that is the result of air raids. Class distinction, dignity, and even financial prestige are hard to maintain in an air-raid shelter at three o'clock in the morning.

And so, as this second year of this war opens, we find the world's greatest army opposing the most powerful navy in the world, with most of the fighting taking place in the air. Europe has suffered much this last twelve months. The next year and the years after that will twist and torture minds and bodies. Reporting Europe will not be a pleasant task. One feels very small and humble. We can only continue to give you the news and the atmosphere in which it happens. You must reach your own conclusions.

VI

September 8 to September 29, 1940

SEPTEMBER 8, 1940. *Marshal Goering takes command of plane attacks on Britain and reports that Germany "now controls the air over Britain."*

SEPTEMBER 11. *Prime Minister Churchill tells House of Commons that Germany is preparing to send an army of invasion by sea.*

SEPTEMBER 14. *United States Congress passes Burke-Wadsworth military conscription bill.*

SEPTEMBER 15. *British claim 185 of 400 German planes downed as against 30 British losses.*

SEPTEMBER 16. *During the past week German planes have damaged 15,000 of the million or more buildings in the London area.*

Italian forces in Egypt occupy Solum and continue twenty-five miles beyond.

SEPTEMBER 23. *British naval squadron withdraws from Dakar after unsuccessful attempt of de Gaulle supporters to persuade local authorities to join Free France.*

SEPTEMBER 24. *British planes drive back two big German bombing attacks before nightfall.*

SEPTEMBER 26. *German planes bomb Southampton heavily while British planes beat their own record in attacks on Channel ports and German cities.*

SEPTEMBER 27. *Germany, Italy, and Japan sign a ten-year-mutual-assistance pact which does not "in any way affect the political status which exists at present as between each of the three contracting parties and Soviet Russia."*

SEPTEMBER 29.   The British assert that the Germans lost 2167
planes and 5418 pilots, gunners, and bombardiers during August and September.

CAN THEY TAKE IT?

[*On September 7, the mass air attacks on London began.*]

SEPTEMBER 8, 1940

Yesterday afternoon—it seems days ago now—I drove down to the East End of London, the East India Dock Road, Commercial Road, through Silvertown, down to the mouth of the Thames Estuary. It was a quiet and almost pleasant trip through those streets running between rows of working-class houses, with the cranes, the docks, the ships, and the oil tanks off on the right. We crossed the river and drove up on a little plateau, which gave us a view from the mouth of the Thames to London. And then an air-raid siren, called "Weeping Willie" by the men who tend it, began its uneven screaming. Down on the coast the white puffballs of antiaircraft fire began to appear against a steel-blue sky. The first flight of German bombers was coming up the river to start the twelve-hour attack against London. They were high and not very numerous. The Hurricanes and Spitfires were already in the air, climbing for altitude above the near-by airdrome. The fight moved inland and out of sight. Things were relatively quiet for about half an hour. Then the British fighters returned. And five minutes later the German bombers, flying in V-formation, began pouring in. The antiaircraft fire was good. Sometimes it

157

seemed to burst right on the nose of the leading machine, but still they came on. On the airdrome, ground crews swarmed over those British fighters, fitting ammunition belts and pouring in gasoline. As soon as one fighter was ready, it took the air, and there was no waiting for flight leaders or formation. The Germans were already coming back, down the river, heading for France.

Up toward London we could see billows of smoke fanning out above the river, and over our heads the British fighters, climbing almost straight up, trying to intercept the bombers before they got away. It went on for two hours and then the "all-clear." We went down to a near-by pub for dinner. Children were already organizing a hunt for bits of shrapnel. Under some bushes beside the road there was a baker's cart. Two boys, still sobbing, were trying to get a quivering bay mare back between the shafts. The lady who ran the pub told us that these raids were bad for the chickens, the dogs, and the horses. A toothless old man of nearly seventy came in and asked for a pint of mild and bitters, confided that he had always, all his life, gone to bed at eight o'clock and found now that three pints of beer made him drowsy-like so he could sleep through any air raid.

Before eight, the siren sounded again. We went back to a haystack near the airdrome. The fires up the river had turned the moon blood red. The smoke had drifted down till it formed a canopy over the Thames; the guns were working all around us, the bursts looking like fireflies in a southern summer night. The Germans were sending in two or three planes at a time, sometimes only one, in relays. They would pass overhead. The guns and lights would follow them, and in about five minutes we could hear the hollow grunt of the bombs. Huge pear-shaped bursts of flame would rise up into the smoke and disappear. The world was upside down. Vincent Sheean lay on one side of me and cursed in five languages; he'd talk about the war in Spain. Ben Robertson, of *PM*, lay on the other side and kept saying over and over in that slow South Carolina drawl, "London is burning, London is burning."

It was like a shuttle service, the way the German planes came up the Thames, the fires acting as a flare path. Often they were above the smoke. The searchlights bored into that black roof, but couldn't penetrate it. They looked like long pillars supporting a black canopy. Suddenly all the lights dashed off and a blackness fell right to the ground. It grew cold. We covered ourselves with hay. The shrapnel clicked as it hit the concrete road near by, and still the German bombers came.

Early this morning we went to a hotel. The gunfire rattled the windows. Shortly before noon we rang for coffee. A pale, red-eyed chambermaid brought it and said, "I hope you slept well, sirs." This afternoon we drove back to the East End of London. It was like an obstacle race—two blocks to the right, then left for four blocks, then straight on for a few blocks, and right again . . . streets roped off, houses and shops smashed . . . a few dirty-faced, tow-headed children standing on a corner, holding their thumbs up, the sign of the men who came back from Dunkerque . . . three red busses drawn up in a line waiting to take the homeless away . . . men with white scarfs around their necks instead of collars and ties, leading dull-eyed, empty-faced women across to the busses. Most of them carried little cheap cardboard suitcases and sometimes bulging paper shopping bags.

That was all they had left. There was still fire and smoke along the river, but the fire fighters and the demolition squads have done their work well.

SEPTEMBER 9, 1940

I've spent the day visiting the bombed areas. The King did the same thing. These people may have been putting on a bold front for the King, but I saw them just as they were—men shoveling mounds of broken glass into trucks, hundreds of people being evacuated from the East End, all of them calm and quiet. In one street where eight or ten houses had been smashed a policeman stopped a motorist who had driven through a red light. The policeman's patience was obviously exhausted. As he made out the ticket and lectured the driver, everyone in the street gathered around to listen, paying no attention at all to the damaged houses; they were much more interested in the policeman.

These people are exceedingly brave, tough, and prudent. The East End, where disaster is always just around the corner, seems to take it better than the more fashionable districts in the West End.

The firemen have done magnificent work these last forty-eight hours. Early this morning I watched them fighting a fire which was obviously being used as a beacon by the German bombers. The bombs came down only a few blocks away, but the firemen just kept their hoses playing steadily at the base of the flame.

The Germans dropped some very big stuff last night. One bomb, which fell about a quarter of a mile from where I was standing on a rooftop, made the largest crater I've ever seen, and I thought I'd seen some big ones. The blast traveled down near-by streets, smashing windows five or six blocks away.

The British shot down three of the night bombers last night. I said a moment ago that Londoners were both brave and prudent. Tonight many theaters are closed. The managers decided the crowds just wouldn't come. Tonight the queues were outside the air-raid shelters, not the theaters. In my district, people carrying blankets and mattresses began going to the shelters before the siren sounded.

This night bombing is serious and sensational. It makes headlines, kills people, and smashes property; but it doesn't win wars. It may be safely presumed that the Germans know that, know that several days of terror bombing will not cause this country to collapse. Where then does this new phase of the air war fit? What happens next? The future must be viewed in relation to previous objectives; those objectives were the western ports and convoys, the Midlands, and Welsh industrial areas, and the southern airfields. And now we have the bombing of London. If this is the prelude to invasion, we must expect much heavier raids against London. After all, they only used about a hundred planes last night. And we must expect a sudden renewal of the attacks against fighter dromes near the coast, an effort to drive the fighters farther inland. If the Germans continue to hammer London for a few more nights and then sweep successfully to blasting airdromes with their dive bombers, it will probably be the signal for invasion. And the currently favored date for this invasion—and you will remember there have been others in the past—is sometime about September 18.

SEPTEMBER 10, 1940—6:45 P.M.

These raids against London are, I think, being rather fully and accurately reported in the United States. Sometimes you get the news a bit late. For instance, when I was talking to you last night I knew all about that big fire down near St. Paul's, had been watching it from a rooftop, but couldn't talk about it. The German planes were still overhead and the Ministry of Home Security had no desire that they should be told, by means of a broadcast to the States, just what fires had been started and where they were. And I might add that I had no desire to assist the German bomb aimers who were flying about over my head. When you hear that London has been bombed and hammered for ten to twelve hours during the night, you should remember that this is a huge, sprawling city, that there is nothing like a continuous rain of bombs—at least, there hasn't been so far. Often there is a period of ten or twenty minutes when no sound can be heard, no searchlights seen. Then a few bombs will come whistling down. Then silence again. A hundred planes over London doesn't mean that they were all here at the same time. They generally come singly or in pairs, circle around over the searchlights two or three times, and then you can hear them start their bombing runs, generally a shallow dive, and those bombs take a long time to fall.

After three nights of watching and listening, these night attacks are assuming something of a pattern for me. The Germans come over as soon as it's dark, a few minutes earlier each night. For the first few hours they drop very little heavy stuff, seem to concentrate on incendiaries, hoping to start fires to act as beacons for the high explosives later on.

CAN THEY TAKE IT?

For the last three nights the weight of the attacks developed around midnight. As you know, the damage has been considerable. But London has suffered no more than a serious flesh wound. The attack will probably increase in intensity, but things will have to get much worse before anyone here is likely to consider it too much to bear.

We are told today that the Germans believe Londoners, after a while, will rise up and demand a new government, one that will make peace with Germany. It's more probable that they'll rise up and murder a few German pilots who come down by parachute. The life of a parachutist would not be worth much in the East End of London tonight.

The politicians who called this a "people's war" were right, probably more right than they knew at the time. I've seen some horrible sights in this city during these days and nights, but not once have I heard man, woman, or child suggest that Britain should throw in her hand. These people are angry. How much they can stand, I don't know. The strain is very great. The prospect for the winter, when some way must be found to keep water out of the shelters and a little heat inside, is not pleasant. Nor will it be any more pleasant in Germany, where winters are generally more severe than on this green island. After four days and nights of this air *Blitzkrieg*, I think the people here are rapidly becoming veterans, even as their Army was hardened in the fire of Dunkerque.

Many people have already got over the panicky feeling that hit everyone in the nerve centers when they realized they were being bombed. Those people I talked to in long queues in front of the big public shelters tonight were cheerful and somewhat resigned. They'd been waiting in line for an hour or more, waiting for the shelters to open at the first wail of the sirens. They had no private shelters of their own, but they carried blankets to throw over the chairs in this public underground refuge. Their sleep tonight will be as fitful as you could expect in such quarters without beds. Of course, they don't like the situation, but most of them feel that even this underground existence is preferable to what they'd get under German domination.

All the while strong efforts are being made to remind the British subjects who live underground that RAF bombers are flying in the other direction and that the Germans are having rather a rough time of it, too. For instance, tonight's British news broadcast led off with a long and detailed statement about last night's RAF air raids against Germany— the docks at Wilhelmshaven, Hamburg, Bremen, and Kiel were bombed again, a power station in Brussels wrecked, and a gasworks on the outskirts of Lorraine set afire. Docks and shipping at Calais, Ostend, Flushing, and Boulogne were also bombed.

SEPTEMBER 10, 1940—10:30 P.M.

This is London. And the raid which started about seven hours ago is still in progress. Larry LeSueur and I have spent the last three hours driving about the streets of London and visiting air-raid shelters. We found that like everything else in this world the kind of protection you get from the bombs on London tonight depends on how much money you have. On the other hand, the most expensive dwelling places here do not necessarily provide the best shelters, but certainly they are the most comfortable.

We looked in on a renowned Mayfair hotel tonight and found many old dowagers and retired colonels settling back on the overstuffed settees in the lobby. It wasn't the sort of protection I'd seek from a direct hit from a half-ton bomb, but if you were a retired colonel and his lady you might feel that the risk was worth it because you would at least be bombed with the right sort of people, and you could always get a drink if you were a resident of the hotel. If you were the sort of person I saw sunk in the padding of this Mayfair mansion you'd be calling for a drink of Scotch and soda pretty often—enough to keep those fine uniformed waiters on the move.

Only a couple of blocks away we pushed aside the canvas curtain of a trench cut out of a lawn of a London park. Inside were half a hundred people, some of them stretched out on the hard wooden benches. The rest huddled over in their overcoats and blankets. Dimmed electric lights glowed on the whitewashed walls and the cannonade of antiaircraft and reverberation of the big stuff the Germans were dropping rattled the dust boards under foot at intervals. You couldn't buy a drink there. One woman was saying sleepily that it was funny how often you read about people being killed inside a shelter. Nobody seemed to listen. Then over to the famous cellar of a world-famous hotel, two floors underground. On upholstered chairs and lounges there was a cosmopolitan crowd. But there wasn't any sparkling cocktail conversation. They sat, some of them with their mouths open. One of them snored. King Zog was over in a far corner on a chair, the porter told me. The woman sleeping on the only cot in the shelter was one of the many sisters of the former King of Albania.

The number of planes engaged tonight seems to be about the same as last night. Searchlight activity has been constant, but there has been little gunfire in the center of London. The bombs have been coming down at about the same rate as last night. It is impossible to get any estimate of the damage. Darkness prevents observation of details. The streets have been deserted save for a few clanging fire engines during the last four or five hours. The zooming planes have been high again tonight, so high that the searchlights can't reach them. The bombing sounds as though it was separated pretty evenly over the metropolitan district. In certain areas there are no electric lights.

Once I saw *The Damnation of Faust* presented in the open air at Salzburg. London reminds me of that tonight, only the stage is so much larger. Once tonight an antiaircraft battery opened fire just as I drove past. It lifted me from the seat and a hot wind swept over the car. It was impossible to see. When I drove on, the streets of London reminded me of a ghost town in Nevada—not a soul to be seen. A week ago there would have been people standing on the corner, shouting for taxis. Tonight there were no people and no taxis. Earlier today there were trucks delivering mattresses to many office buildings. People are now sleeping on those mattresses, or at least they are trying to sleep. The coffee stalls, where taxi drivers and truck drivers have their four-in-the-morning tea, are empty.

As I entered this building half an hour ago one man was asking another if he had a good book. He was offered a mystery story, something about a woman who murdered her husband. And as he stumbled sleepily down the corridor, the lender said, "Hope it doesn't keep you awake."

And so London is waiting for dawn. We ought to get the "all-clear" in about another two hours. Then those big German bombers that have been lumbering and mumbling about overhead all night will have to go home.

SEPTEMBER 11, 1940

The air raid is still on. I shall speak rather softly, because three or four people are sleeping on mattresses on the floor of this studio.

The latest official figures for today's air war list at least ninety German planes down, with a loss of seventeen British fighters.

It is now 4:15 in the morning in London. There will be piles of empty shell casings around London's antiaircraft batteries when dawn breaks about an hour from now. All night, for more than eight hours, the guns have been flashing. The blue of an autumn sky has been pockmarked with the small red burst of exploding antiaircraft shells. Never in the long history of this old city beside the Thames has there been such a night as this. But tonight the sound of gunfire has been more constant than the bestial grunt of bombs.

Several hours of observation from a rooftop in central London has convinced me that the bombing of the central and western portion of the city has been less severe than during last night, and tomorrow's official communiqué will confirm that impression. The number of German planes engaged has probably been about the same—something more than a hundred. Most of the bombings have been over near the river. Judging from the height of the shell bursts, the Germans have been bombing from a somewhat lower altitude tonight. They cruise at about the same height, but when they start their bombing runs, the bursts appear lower down. A few fires have been started, but most of them are believed to be under control.

These London gunners, who have spent the better part of a year sitting around doing nothing, are working tonight. There's a battery not far from where I live. They're working in their shirt sleeves, laughing and cursing as they slam the shells into their guns. The spotters and detectors swing slowly around in their reclining carriage. The lens of the night glasses look like the eyes of an overgrown owl in the orange-blue light that belches from the muzzle of the gun. They're working without searchlights tonight. The moon is so bright that the beam of the light is lost a few hundred feet off the ground. Someone should paint the chimney pots and gables of London as they're silhouetted in the flashing flame of the guns, when the world seems upside down.

Walking down the street a few minutes ago, shrapnel stuttered and stammered on the rooftops and from underground came the sound of singing, and the song was *My Blue Heaven*.

Here's a story of a policeman, his whistle, and a time bomb. It's a true story. I saw it. If the story lacks literary merit, put it down to the fact that composition is not easy when your windows are being rattled by gunfire and bombs. In the central district of London a bomb fell. It didn't explode. The area was roped off. People living in the area were evacuated—moved out of the buildings. I happened to be walking in that particular district and talked my way just inside the police cordon. Peering fearfully around the corner of a stout building, I beheld a policeman standing at an intersection, about thirty yards from where that unexploded bomb lay. He was a big policeman—his feet were wide apart, tin hat pushed well back on his head, chin strap between his teeth, left hand hooked in his belt at the back. That policeman's right hand snapped up from the wrist. Something glinted in the sunlight and dropped back into his hand. Again that slow, easy flick of the wrist. And I saw he had taken his whistle off the chain, was tossing it idly in the air and catching it as it fell. It was an effortless, mechanical sort of business. He stood like a statue, just tossing that silver whistle and catching it. I've seen cops at home perform something of the same operation with a night stick on a warm spring day. If that bomb had gone off, the bobby would have been a dead man, the whistle would have fallen to the pavement.

After watching him for perhaps two minutes I withdrew, convinced that it would have been impossible for me to catch that whistle in a washtub. What the policeman was doing there, I don't know. He may be there still.

These delayed-action bombs create special problems. If a bomb explodes in a business district, it may do considerable damage, but demolition and repair work can be started at once. Offices and shops that have escaped damage can carry on. But a delayed-action bomb can paralyze the area for a considerable time. If a bomb explodes on a railway line, only a few hours may be required to effect repairs; but a time bomb on a right of way is more difficult to deal with. Anyone can fill in a bomb crater, but experts are required to handle the ones that don't explode.

I know of a case where there was an unexploded bomb

between the rails. The local superintendent organized a volunteer crew to take a freight train over it. But when the freight arrived, the regular crew refused to hand it over to the volunteers. They said the locals could have the bomb, but they'd take the train through. They did and, luckily, the bomb didn't explode.

Military medals are getting rather meaningless in this war. So many acts of heroism are being performed by men who were just doing their daily job. And now at 4:20 in the morning we're just waiting for the "all-clear."

SEPTEMBER 12, 1940

Miss Dorothy Thompson made a broadcast to Britain tonight. Her audience was somewhat reduced, since the air-raid siren sounded just after she started speaking. She informed the British that the poets of the world were lined up on their side. That, she said, was a matter of consequence. I'm not sure that Londoners agreed that the poets would be of much assistance, as they grabbed their blankets and headed for the air-raid shelters. I think these Londoners put more faith in their antiaircraft barrage, which seemed to splash blobs of daylight down the streets tonight. Hitler, said Miss Thompson, wants to destroy the mental and spiritual heritage of free peoples. She promised the British that they would win. She said they had never been so beloved. She predicted that ages from now mothers and fathers would gather their children about their knees and tell them about these days. Well, mothers and fathers have their children about them tonight—underground. They're sustained in part by folklore, the tradition, and the history of Britain; but they're an undemonstrative lot. They don't consider themselves to be heroes. There's a job of work to be done and they're doing it as best they can. They don't know themselves how long they can stand up to it.

I know something about these Londoners. They know that they're out on their own. Most of them expect little help from the poets and no effective defense by word of mouth. These black-faced men with bloodshot eyes who were fighting fires and the girls who cradled the steering wheel of a heavy ambulance in their arms, the policeman who stands guards over that unexploded bomb down at St. Paul's tonight—these people didn't hear Miss Thompson; they're busy, just doing a job of work, and they know that it all depends on them.

SEPTEMBER 13, 1940

This is London at three-thirty in the morning. This has been what might be called a "routine night"—air-raid alarm at about nine o'clock and intermittent bombing ever since. I had the impression that more high explosives and few incendiaries have been used tonight. Only two small fires can be seen on the horizon. Again the Germans have been sending their bombers in singly or in pairs. The antiaircraft barrage has been fierce but sometimes there have been periods of twenty minutes when London has been silent. Then the big red busses would start up and move on till the guns started working again. That silence is almost hard to bear. One becomes accustomed to rattling windows and the distant sound of bombs and then there comes a silence that can be felt. You know the sound will return—you wait, and then it starts again. That waiting is bad. It gives you a chance to imagine things. I have been walking tonight—there is a full moon, and the dirty-gray buildings appear white. The stars, the empty windows, are hidden. It's a beautiful and lonesome city where men and women and children are trying to snatch a few hours' sleep underground.

In the fashionable residential districts I could read the TO LET signs on the front of big houses in the light of the bright moon. Those houses have big basements underneath —good shelters, but they're not being used. Many people think they should be.

The scale of this air war is so great that the reporting of it is not easy. Often we spend hours traveling about this sprawling city, viewing damage, talking with people, and occasionally listening to the bombs come down, and then more hours wondering what you'd like to hear about these people who are citizens of no mean city. We've told you about the bombs, the fires, the smashed houses, and the courage of the people. We've read you the communiqués and tried to give you an honest estimate of the wounds inflicted upon this, the best bombing target in the world. But the business of living and working in this city is very personal—the little incidents, the things the mind retains, are in themselves unimportant, but they somehow weld together to form the hard core of memories that will remain when the last "all-clear" has sounded. That's why I want to talk for just three or four minutes about the things we haven't talked about before; for many of these impressions it is necessary to reach back through only one long week. There was a rainbow bending over the battered and smoking East End of London just when the "all-clear" sounded one afternoon. One night I stood in front of a smashed grocery store and heard a dripping inside. It was the only sound in all London. Two cans of peaches had been drilled clean through by flying glass and the juice was dripping down onto the floor.

There was a flower shop in the East End. Nearly every other building in the block had been smashed. There was a funeral wreath in the window of the shop—price: three shillings and six pence, less than a dollar. In front of Buckingham Palace there's a bed of red and white flowers—untouched—the reddest flowers I've ever seen.

Last night, or rather early this morning, I met a distinguished member of Parliament in a bar. He had been dining with Anthony Eden and had told the Secretary for War that he wouldn't walk through the streets with all that shrapnel falling about and as a good host Eden should send him home in a tank. Another man came in and reported, on good authority, that the Prime Minister had a siren suit, one of those blue woolen coverall affairs with a zipper. Someone said the Prime Minister must resemble a barrage balloon when attired in his siren suit. Things of that sort can still be said in this country. The fact that the noise— just the sound, not the blast—of bombs and guns can cause one to stagger while walking down the street came as a surprise. When I entered my office today, after bombs had fallen two blocks away, and was asked by my English secretary if I'd care for a cup of tea, that didn't come as much of a surprise.

Talking from a studio with a few bodies lying about on the floor, sleeping on mattresses, still produces a strange feeling but we'll probably get used to that. Today I went to buy a hat—my favorite shop had gone, blown to bits. The windows of my shoe store were blown out. I decided to have a haircut; the windows of the barbershop were gone, but the Italian barber was still doing business. Someday, he said, we smile again, but the food it doesn't taste so good since being bombed. I went on to another shop to buy flashlight batteries. I bought three. The clerk said: "You needn't buy so many. We'll have enough for the whole winter." But I said: "What if you aren't here?" There were buildings down in that street, and he replied: "Of course, we'll be here. We've been in business here for a hundred and fifty years."

But the sundown scene in London can never be forgotten —the time when people pick up their beds and walk to the shelter.

SEPTEMBER 15, 1940

During the last week you have heard much of the bombing of Buckingham Palace and probably seen pictures of the damage. You have been told by certain editors and commentators who sit in New York that the bombing of the Palace, which has one of the best air-raid shelters in England, caused a great surge of determination—a feeling of unity—to sweep this island. The bombing was called a great psychological blunder. I do not find much support for that point of view amongst Londoners with whom I've talked. They don't like the idea of their King and Queen being bombed, but, remember, this is not the last war—people's reactions are different. Minds have become hardened and callused. It didn't require a bombing of Buckingham Palace to convince these people that they are all in this thing together. There is nothing exclusive about being bombed these days. When there are houses down in your street, when friends and relatives have been killed, when you've seen that red glow in the sky night after night, when you're tired and sleepy—there just isn't enough energy left to be outraged about the bombing of a palace.

The King and Queen have earned the respect and admiration of the nation, but so have tens of thousands of humble folk who are much less well protected. If the Palace had been the only place bombed the reaction might have been different. Maybe some of those German bomb aimers are working for Goebbels instead of Goering, but if the purpose of the bombings was to strike terror to the hearts of the Britishers then the bombs have been wasted. That fire bomb on the House of Lords passed almost unnoticed. I heard a parcel of people laughing about it when one man said: "That particular bomb wouldn't seriously have damaged the nation's war effort."

I'm talking about those things not because the bombing of the Palace appears to have affected America more than Britain, but in order that you may understand that this war has no relation with the last one, so far as symbols and civilians are concerned. You must understand that a world is dying, that old values, the old prejudices, and the old bases of power and prestige are going. In an army, if the morale is to be good, there must be equality in the ranks. The private with money must not be allowed to buy himself a shelter of steel and concrete in the front-line trench. One company can't be equipped with pitchforks and another with machine guns. London's civilian army doesn't have that essential equality—I mean equality of shelter. One borough before the war defied the authorities and built deep shelters. Now people arrive at those shelters from all over town and the people who paid for them are in danger of being crowded out. Some of those outsiders arrive in taxis, others by foot. Since it's a public shelter they can't be barred by the people whose money went into the digging. This is just one of the problems in equality that London is now facing.

There are the homeless from the bombed and fire-blackened East End area. They must be cared for, they must be moved, they must be fed, and they must be sheltered. The Lord Mayor's fund, contributions from America, from unofficial agencies, are in the best tradition of Anglo-Saxon generosity and philanthropy, but no general would desire to rely upon such measures for the care and maintenance of injured troops. The people have been told that this is a people's war, that they are in the front lines, and they are. If morale is to be maintained at its present high level, there must be no distinction between the troops living in the various sections of London.

Even for those of us who live on the crest of London, life is dangerous. Some of the old buildings have gone, but the ghosts, sometimes a whole company of ghosts, remain. There is the thunder of gunfire at night. As these lines were written, as the window shook, there was a candle and matches beside the typewriter just in case the light went out. Richard Llewellyn, the man who wrote *How Green Was My Valley*, sat in the corner and talked about the dignity of silence while the guns jarred the apartment house. We went out to dinner and the headwaiter carefully placed us at a table away from the window. "There might be," he said, "one of those blasts." In the West End of London, life follows some kind of pattern. The shops are still full of food; the milk arrives on the doorstep each morning; the papers, too, but sometimes they're a little late. Much of the talk, as you would expect, is about invasion. On that score there is considerable confidence. Everyone is convinced that it will be beaten back if it comes. There are some who fear that it will not come.

SEPTEMBER 18, 1940

I'd like to say one or two things about the reporting of this air war against London. No one person can see it all. The communiqués are sparing of information because details of damage would assist the Germans. No one can check by personal observation the damage done during a single night or a single week. It would take a lifetime to traverse the streets of this city, but there's a greater problem involved; it's one of language. There are no words to describe the thing that is happening. Today I talked with eight American correspondents in London. Six of them had been forced to move—all had stories of bombs and all agreed that they were unable to convey through print or the spoken word an accurate impression of what's happening in London these days and nights.

I may tell you that Bond Street has been bombed; that a shop selling handkerchiefs at $40 the dozen has been wrecked; that these words were written on a table of good English oak which sheltered me three times as bombs tore down in the vicinity, but you can have little understanding of the life in London these days—the courage of the people;

the flash and roar of the guns rolling down streets where much of the history of the English-speaking world has been made; the stench of air-raid shelters in the poor districts. These things must be experienced to be understood.

A woman inspecting a sweater, taking it to the bright sunlight shining through a smashed skylight for close inspection. A row of automobiles, with stretchers racked on the roofs like skis, standing outside of bombed buildings. A man pinned under wreckage where a broken gas main sears his arm and face. These things must be seen if the whole impact of this war is to be felt.

If we talk at times of the little flashes of humor that appear in this twilight of suffering, you must understand that there is humor in these people, even when disaster and hell come down from heaven. We can only tell you what we see and hear.

The individual's reaction to the sound of falling bombs cannot be described. The moan of stark terror and suspense cannot be encompassed by words, no more can the sense of relief when you realize that you weren't where that one fell. It's pleasant to pick yourself up out of the gutter without the aid of a searcher party.

Between bombing one catches glimpses of the London one knew in the distant days of peace. The big red busses roll through the streets. The tolling of Big Ben can be heard in the intervals of the gunfire. The little French and Italian restaurants in Soho bring out their whitest linens and polish their glass and silver for the two or three guests who brave the blackout, the bombs, and the barrage. There are advertisements in the papers extolling the virtues of little rubber ear plugs which prevent one from hearing the bombs and guns. In many buildings tonight people are sleeping on mattresses on the floor. I've seen dozens of them looking like dolls thrown aside by a tired child. In three or four hours they must get up and go to work just as though they had had a full night's rest, free from the rumble of guns and the wonder that comes when they wake and listen in the dead hours of the night.

SEPTEMBER 21, 1940

I'm standing on a rooftop looking out over London. At the moment everything is quiet. For reasons of national as well as personal security, I'm unable to tell you the exact location from which I'm speaking. Off to my left, far away in the distance, I can see just that faint-red, angry snap of antiaircraft bursts against the steel-blue sky, but the guns are so far away that it's impossible to hear them from this location. About five minutes ago the guns in the immediate vicinity were working. I can look across just at a building not far away and see something that looks like a flash of white paint down the side, and I know from daylight observation that about a quarter of that building has disappeared —hit by a bomb the other night. Streets fan out in all directions from here, and down on one street I can see a single red light and just faintly the outline of a sign standing in the middle of the street. And again I know what that sign says, because I saw it this afternoon. It says DANGER—UNEX-PLODED BOMB. Off to my left still I can see just that red snap of the antiaircraft fire.

I was up here earlier this afternoon and looking out over these housetops, looking all the way to the dome of St. Paul's. I saw many flags flying from staffs. No one ordered these people to put out the flag. They simply feel like flying the Union Jack above their roof. No one told them to do it, and no flag up there was white. I can see one or two of them just stirring very faintly in the breeze now. You may be able to hear the sound of guns off in the distance very faintly, like someone kicking a tub. Now they're silent. Four searchlights reach up, disappear in the light of a three-quarter moon. I should say at the moment there are probably three aircraft in the general vicinity of London, as one can tell by the movement of the lights and the flash of the antiaircraft guns. But at the moment in the central area everything is quiet. More searchlights spring up over on my right. I think probably in a minute we shall have the sound of guns in the immediate vicinity. The lights are swinging over in this general direction now. You'll hear two explosions. There they are! That was the explosion overhead, not the guns themselves. I should think in a few minutes there may be a bit of shrapnel around here. Coming in—moving a little closer all the while. The plane's still very high. Earlier this evening we could hear occasional . . . again those were explosions overhead. Earlier this evening we heard a number of bombs go sliding and slithering across to fall several blocks away. Just overhead now the burst of the anti-aircraft fire. Still the near-by guns are not working. The searchlights now are feeling almost directly overhead. Now you'll hear two bursts a little nearer in a moment. There they are! That hard, stony sound.

SEPTEMBER 22, 1940

I'm standing again tonight on a rooftop looking out over London, feeling rather large and lonesome. In the course of the last fifteen or twenty minutes there's been considerable action up there, but at the moment there's an ominous silence hanging over London. But at the same time a silence that has a great deal of dignity. Just straightaway in front of me the searchlights are working. I can see one or two bursts of antiaircraft fire far in the distance. Just on the roof across the way I can see a man standing wearing a tin hat, with a pair of powerful night glasses to his eyes, scanning the sky. Again looking in the opposite direction there is a building with two windows gone. Out of one window there waves something that looks like a white bed sheet, a window curtain swinging free in this night breeze. It looks as though it were being shaken by a ghost. There are a great many ghosts around these buildings in London. The search-lights straightaway, miles in front of me, are still scratching that sky. There's a three-quarter moon riding high. There was one burst of shellfire almost straight in the Little Dipper. The guns are too far away to be heard.

Down below in the streets I can see just that red and green wink of the traffic lights; one lone taxicab moving slowly down the street. Not a sound to be heard. As I look out across the miles and miles of rooftops and chimney pots, some of those dirty-gray fronts of the buildings look almost snow white in this moonlight here tonight. And the rooftop spotter across the way swings around, looks over in the direction of the searchlights, drops his glasses, and just stands there. There are hundreds and hundreds of men like

that standing on rooftops in London tonight watching for
fire bombs, waiting to see what comes out of this steel-blue
sky. The searchlights now reach up very, very faintly on
three sides of me. There is a flash of a gun in the distance,
but too far away to be heard.

SEPTEMBER 23, 1940

This is London, about ten minutes to four in the morning. Tonight's raid which started about eight is still in progress. The number of planes engaged is about the same as
usual, perhaps a few more than last night. Barring lucky
hits, both damage and casualties should be no greater than
on previous nights. The next three hours may bring a
change, but so far the raid appears to be routine, with the
Germans flying perhaps a little lower than they did last
night.

Often we wonder what you'd like to hear from London
at four in the morning. There's seldom any spot news after
midnight, so we just talk about the city and its people.
Today I went to our district post office. There was a long
line of people waiting for their mail. Their offices or homes
had been bombed, and the mailman couldn't find them.
There were no complaints. But that's not quite right. One
woman said: "They've got to stop this; it can't go on." Her
neighbor said: "Have you ever thought what would happen
to you if we gave in?" And the lady replied, "Yes, I know,
but have you seen what happened to Peter Robinson's?"
Others in the queue—those who've been called by Mr.
Churchill the more robust elements of the community—
silenced the lady with well-modulated laughter.

To me one of the most impressive things about talking with Londoners these days is this—there's no mention of money. No one knows the dollar value of the damage done during these last sixteen days. But nobody talks about it. People who've had their homes or offices bombed will tell you about it, but they never think to tell you what the loss amounted to, whether it was so many tens or hundreds of pounds. The lead of any well-written news story dealing with fire, flood, or hurricane should tell something of the total damage done in terms of dollars, but here it's much more important that the bomb missed you; that there's still plenty of food to eat—and there is.

My own apartment is in one of the most heavily bombed areas of London, but the newspapers are on the doorstep each morning—so is the bottle of milk. When the light switch is pressed, there is light, and the gas stove still works, and they're still building that house across the street, still putting in big windowpanes. Today I saw shopwindows in Oxford Street, covered with plywood. In front of one there was a redheaded girl in a blue smock, painting a sign on the board covering the place where the window used to be. The sign read OPEN AS USUAL. A block away men were working an air hammer, breaking up huge blocks of masonry that had been blown into the streets, cracking those big lumps so that they might be carted away in trucks.

The people who have something to do with their hands are all right. Action seems to drive out fear. Those who have nothing to do would be better off outside London and there are signs that they will be encouraged to go. London comes to resemble a small town. There's something of a frontier atmosphere about the place. The other night I saw half a block evacuated. Time bombs plus incendiaries did it. In half an hour the people who had been turned out of their homes had been absorbed in near-by houses and apartments. Those who arranged for the influx of unexpected guests had, I think, been frightened when those bombs came down, but they were all right when there was something to do. Blankets to get out of closets, tea to be made, and all that sort of thing.

I've talked to firemen fighting a blaze that was being used as a beacon by German bomb aimers. They told me that the waiting about in fire stations was worst of all. They didn't mind the danger when there was something to do. Even my censor when I arrived in the studio tonight was sitting here underground composing music.

A half an hour before the King made his broadcast tonight the air-raid alarm sounded. At that moment a man with a deep voice was telling the children of Britain by radio how the wasps build their nests. He said, "Good night, children everywhere." There was a brief prayer for the children who went down in mid-Atlantic last week. There was a hymn well sung. After that a piano playing some nursery song, I didn't know it's name. There was a moment of silence. Then the words, "This is London, His Majesty, the King." The King spoke for half a minute and then the welcome sound of the "all-clear," that high, steady note of the siren, came rolling through the open window. One almost expected His Majesty to pause and let the welcome sound come out through the loudspeaker, but he probably didn't hear it since he was speaking from an air-raid shelter under Buckingham Palace. The only news in the King's speech was the announcement of the two new medals, but his warning of grimmer days ahead must be taken as another indication of government policy—a warning that the full weight of German bombing is yet to be experienced.

Since the disastrous retreat from Norway, the government has been issuing few sunshine statements. Nearly every statement has been couched in subtle language, has contained a warning of worse things to come.

And now the King has added his warning to those of his ministers. He took the advice of his ministers, as he must, in speaking as he did, and his ministers judged, and rightly, that these people can stand up to that sort of warning. There has been much talk of terror bombings, but it is clear that London has not yet experienced anything like the full power of the *Luftwaffe* in these night raids. The atmosphere for full-scale terror bombing is not right. There is as yet no sizable portion of the population prepared to talk terms with the Nazis. You must remember that this war is being fought with political as well as military weapons. If the time comes when the Germans believe that mass night raids will break this government, then we may see German bombers quartering this night sky in an orgy of death and destruction such as no modern city has ever seen. There are no available official figures, but I have watched these planes night after night and do not believe that more than one hundred and fifty have been used in any single night. The Germans have more planes than that. Sometime they may use them. The people had to be warned about that. Therefore, the King spoke as he did.

SEPTEMBER 25, 1940

This is London, 3:45 in the morning. Tonight's attack against the central London area has not been as severe as last night; less noise, fewer bombs, and not so many fires. The night is almost quiet—almost peaceful. The raid is still in progress and it is, of course, possible that we may see a repetition of last night when the weight of the attack developed in the two hours before dawn. Two and sometimes three German planes came boring in through the barrage every five minutes. I spent last night with a bomber pilot who had carried twenty-five loads of bombs over Germany. He talked about a raid over Berlin at this time last night. When we left the studio we'd gone only a few blocks when we heard one coming down. As we lay on the sidewalk waiting for it to thump, he said, "I'd feel better up there than down there." A couple of air-raid wardens standing out in the open were discussing whether the stuff coming down was a flock of incendiaries or high explosives. The bomber pilot said: "These people are too brave. I'll feel better when I get back to my squadron. London is dangerous. I wonder how long it takes to get used to this sort of thing."

Later we went out to see a fire. A block of cheap little working-class houses had been set alight by fire bombs. As we walked toward the blaze, gusts of hot air and sparks charged down the street. We began to meet women. One clutched a blanket, another carried a small baby in her arms, and another carried an aluminum cooking pot in her left hand. They were all looking back over their shoulders at that red glow that had driven them out into the streets. They were frightened. And that bomber pilot who had been over Germany so many times stopped and said: "I've seen enough of this. I hope we haven't been doing the same thing in the Ruhr and Rhineland for the last three months."

We went back to a rooftop and stood watching as the bombers came in. He estimated their height, the speed at which they were traveling, and the point at which they would release their bombs. And he was generally right as to the time when we would hear the bombs start coming down. He was a professional, judging the work of other professionals. But he kept talking of the firemen, the ambulance drivers, and the air-raid wardens who were out there doing their job. He thought them much braver than the boys who'd been flying over Germany every night.

At dawn we saw Londoners come oozing up out of the ground, tired, red-eyed, and sleepy. The fires were dying down. We saw them turn into their own street and look to see if their house was still standing. I shall always wonder what last night did to that twenty-one-year-old boy who had flown so many bombs over Germany but had never heard one come down before last night. Today I walked down a long street. The gutters were full of glass; the big red busses couldn't pull into the curb. There was the harsh, grating sound of glass being shoveled into trucks. In one window— or what used to be a window—was a sign. It read: SHATTERED—BUT NOT SHUTTERED. Near by was another shop displaying a crudely lettered sign reading: KNOCKED BUT NOT LOCKED. They were both doing business in the open air. Halfway down the block there was a desk on the sidewalk; a man sat behind it with a pile of notes at his elbow. He was paying off the staff of the store—the store that stood there yesterday.

I went to my club for lunch. A neatly lettered sign on the door informed me that the club had been temporarily closed, due to enemy action. Returning to my apartment, which is now serving as an office, I found a letter from the China Campaign Committee, informing me that during the last fifteen days they had collected the signatures of individuals and organizations representing more than one and a quarter million people. The signatures were attached to a petition. The petition read as follows: "We demand the immediate and unconditional reopening of the Burma Road." It is necessary to have lived these last fifteen days in Britain to fully appreciate that letter. Collecting signatures to a petition urging the opening of the Burma Road during fifteen days of almost constant air-raid alarms. The petition was started before the *Blitzkrieg*. Therefore, it had to be carried through. These people are stubborn. Often they are insular, but their determination must be recorded.

SEPTEMBER 29, 1940

Tonight I can give you some idea of what it's like to get away from it all, away from the bombs, the guns, and the strained faces. I have spent nearly two days down in West Somerset. That's near the Bristol Channel. The train left from a station that has been burned and bombed by Dr. Goebbels, but I couldn't see any signs of damage. Dinner on the train was as usual. The coffee was still undrinkable, and the cheese is just cheese. It doesn't masquerade under such fancy names as Gorgonzola or Stilton. But they still serve those little red radishes with it. We were only fifteen minutes late at the end of a four-hour trip. Then half an hour by car to a little village tucked away at the end of a finger of salt water. A dozen houses and a tiny little hotel. A row of red geraniums standing guard in front of a white-washed stone wall. The landlord said, "You'll sleep well to-night." But I didn't. At night a gentle breeze off the Channel nibbled and scratched at the thatched roof outside my window. It sounded like incendiary coming down. The swish of gravel on the beach as each wave retreated resembled that distant sound of falling brick and mortar after a bomb explosion. The clang of ironshod horses' hoofs on stone road was like distant gunfire, but it was only the mounted night patrol riding up to Exmoor, lying brown and wrinkled like a carpet mountain behind the hotel. That's hunting and shooting country down there and they take their night patrol seriously.

At eight in the morning a German bomber crashed on the beach three hundred yards from the hotel. Three members of the crew walked out. The fourth was dead. The three Germans were taken away across the fields in a small car with an armed horseman in front and another behind. It was the first time the war had come to the village. There was great excitement. The bar did a rushing business. The tide came in and covered the twin-engined bomber. The bombing of London, the progress of the war, were forgotten. You must remember there had been only two air-raid alarms in the village during the year. An old lady said she was sorry the Germans had discovered her village. I walked across the moors on grass that seemed to have springs for roots to a little village beside a stream. There was an old Roman footbridge across the stream. The name of the hotel was the Royal Oak. The landlord provided a huge tea, thick cream, and all the rest. He explained that he had enough food to last a year even if nothing came in, offered me a pork sandwich. I said, "I thought you weren't allowed to kill pigs under the new government order." "That's right," he said, "but sometimes they have accidents. This one caught his hind legs in a gate and we had to kill him." His wife wanted to know about London, but the landlord forestalled my answer by saying, "They'll be all right. I was worried about 'em for a couple of days, but they've got their teeth into this thing now, and they'll be all right." And then looking at his snug little hotel and up at the brown slopes of Exmoor, he said a strange thing. He said, "It's too bad some people have to live in terror and fear, being bombed every night, when nothing happens to us. If we could spread it out a bit, all share in it, maybe it wouldn't be so bad." And then I understood what people mean when they say this country is united.

The local paper was already advising people to do their Christmas shopping early, assuring them that large stocks were available, and judging from the appearance of the shopwindows, the paper was right. The paper also reported the meeting of the town council. The session was, I gathered, devoted to a discussion of the street-lighting system installed several years ago. Certain standing charges were still due annually to the public-utility company, in spite of the fact that the lights were, of course, no longer used. One town counselor had said, apparently in all seriousness, that a neighboring town had showed much more foresight, hadn't gone in for this new business of installing street lights.

Everywhere I noticed a change in people's faces. There

was no strain. There was color given by sun and wind. They told me how the beech hedges lining the roads that snaked across the moor were cut back every fourteen years and it would soon be time to cut them back again. The harvest was early this year, and now the farmers have a few slack weeks and a chance to attend the autumn sale. And all the time as I listened to those soft voices down in the Lorna Doone country, I kept wondering what was happening in London. So, late in the evening, a train brought me back to London. As we neared the outskirts, the conductor came in, turned out the lights, and said apologetically, "I'm afraid there's an air raid on." Arrived at the station, I found a taxi, gave the aged driver the address, and he said, "Right you are, sir. I 'ope it's still there."

It's a strange feeling to ride through dark streets lit by the flash of antiaircraft fire, wondering whether your home is still standing or whether it has become a pile of ruined rubble during your brief absence. All was well. Somehow I thought London would have changed, but it seemed the same. The night raid is still on. The hours away from the city have evaporated. As the man who shared my taxi remarked, "It's like coming back to the front lines after a short leave."

October 3 to December 27, 1940

OCTOBER 3, 1940. *Neville Chamberlain resigns from the Church-ill Cabinet and the next day retires as leader of the Conservative party.*

OCTOBER 27. *Italian warplanes attack Greece across Albanian frontier after Greece rejects three-hour Italian ultimatum.*

OCTOBER 30. *Italian High Command announces, "Our troops have continued to advance into Greek territory, overcoming resistance on the enemy's rear guard."*

NOVEMBER 3. *Greeks launch Koritza counteroffensive.*

NOVEMBER 5. *Prime Minister Churchill announces that the government of Eire has refused several British requests for naval and air bases.*

NOVEMBER 11. *The Royal Air Force announces that repeated raids on Hamburg have caused extensive damage to industry.*

NOVEMBER 12. *British aircraft attack Italian war vessels in Taranto and seriously damage several large battleships.*

NOVEMBER 15. *German planes launch mass night attack on city of Coventry, killing more than 200 people and wounding over 800.*

NOVEMBER 16. *The Greek High Command reports Italians evacuating their base at Koritza in Albania.*

NOVEMBER 23. *Rumania joins German-Italian-Japanese alliance.*

DECEMBER 6. *Italian retreats continue as Greeks capture Porto Edda and Marshal Badoglio resigns as chief of staff.*

DECEMBER 11. *On second day of offensive against Italians in*

Egypt, the British and Imperial Army of the Nile take Sidi Barrani and thousands of prisoners.

DECEMBER 14.   Pétain ousts Laval from the French Cabinet.

DECEMBER 15.   British drive all Italians from Egypt and pursue them into Libya.

DECEMBER 23.   Lord Halifax appointed British Ambassador to the United States to replace Lord Lothian who died on December 12.

DECEMBER 27.   British and Germans renew bombings after Christmas truce.

VII

THEY CAN TAKE IT

OCTOBER 1, 1940

Here are one or two impressions picked up during the last week, conclusions drawn from reading and from knowing many of the men who have done the writing and, above all else, from listening. The British have a rather curious ability to wipe the slate clean. Their memories are short. Defeats are unpleasant and therefore best quickly forgotten. Their ability to stand bad news is astounding. The latest withdrawal, from Dakar, has been pretty well forgotten by the average man, but there are still many questions to be answered about that expedition. There is some impatience that the Prime Minister has not made a statement on the subject, that the House of Commons has not been called. Some criticism of the frequent secret sessions of the House. Many people here believe that France would not have capitulated had the Chamber of Deputies been in session. There is considerable contempt for the present French government and a widespread belief that it can't possibly represent the will of the French people. But there is also a tendency to underrate the importance of what is happening on the Continent, a sort of feeling that sometime, somehow, France will return to her former ways. There is a failure to recognize that there can be no return without revolution, and the British government is not geared to revolutionary thought or action or the fomenting of revolution abroad. Great powers have been vested in His Majesty's government, but in Parliament the majority is still held by the Conservative party under the leadership of Mr. Chamberlain. There is a so-called dictator for the homeless, but his powers are strictly limited. In this war against civilians, a war where the armed forces worry about the folks at home instead of the people at home worrying about the troops at the front, organization counts and speed is king.

There is occurring in this country a revolution by consent. Millions of people ask only, "What can we do to help? Why must there be 800,000 unemployed when we need these shelters? Why can't the unemployed miners dig? Why are new buildings being constructed when the need is that the wreckage of bombed buildings be removed from the streets? What are the war aims of this country? What shall we do with victory when it's won? What sort of Europe will be build when and if this stress has passed?" These questions are being asked by thoughtful people in this country. Mark it down that in the three weeks of the air *blitz* against this country more books and pamphlets have been published on these subjects than in any similar period of the war. Remember also that I am permitted to record this plan of political and social salvation at a time when this country fights for its life. Mark it down that these people are both brave and patient, that all are equal under the bomb, that this is a war of speed and organization, and that the political system which best provides for the defense and decency of the little man will win. You are witnessing the beginning of a revolution, maybe the death of an age. All these moves, Dakar, the pact with Japan, diplomats flying hither and yon, mean only that a large section of the world is waiting to be told what to do, as the Germans were waiting seven years ago.

Today, in one of the most famous streets in London, I saw soldiers at work clearing away the wreckage of nearly an entire block. The men were covered with white dust. Some of them wore goggles to protect their eyes. They thought maybe people were still buried in the basement. The sirens sounded, and still they tore at the beams and bricks covering the place where the basements used to be. They are still working tonight. I saw them after tonight's raid started. They paid no attention to the bursts of anti-aircraft fire overhead as they bent their backs and carried away basketfuls of mortar and brick. A few small steam shovels would help them considerably in digging through those ruins. But all the modern instruments seem to be overhead. Down here on the ground people must work with their hands.

OCTOBER 4, 1940

In this evening's London papers, President Nicholas Murray Butler, of Columbia University, is quoted as saying that any faculty member who cannot agree with the university's stand and its desire to help Britain should resign. That will make strange reading to British scholars. No university head in this country had made such a pronouncement. Even in wartime, it's not customary for scholars to demand that their colleagues share their political and international views. It's still possible for British professors to pursue the search for truth without dictation. The theory is that the dissenters will be dealt with and argued with by the more robust elements of the academic community. Maybe the British are too tolerant, but it must be remembered that that tolerance has produced a pretty high degree of national unity.

OCTOBER 10, 1940

This is London, ten minutes before five in the morning. Tonight's raid has been widespread. London is again the main target. Bombs have been reported from more than fifty districts. Raiders have been over Wales in the west, the Midlands, Liverpool, the southwest, and northeast. So far as London is concerned, the outskirts appear to have suffered the heaviest pounding. The attack has decreased in intensity since the moon faded from the sky.

All the fires were quickly brought under control. That's a common phrase in the morning communiqués. I've seen how it's done; spent a night with the London fire brigade. For three hours after the night attack got going, I shivered in a sandbag crow's-nest atop a tall building near the Thames. It was one of the many fire-observation posts. There was an old gun barrel mounted above a round table marked off like a compass. A stick of incendairies bounced off rooftops about three miles away. The observer took a sight on a point where the first one fell, swung his gun sight along the line of bombs, and took another reading at the end of the line of fire. Then he picked up his telephone and shouted above the half gale that was blowing up there, "Stick of incendiaries—between 190 and 220—about three miles away." Five minutes later a German bomber came boring down the river. We could see his exhaust trail like a pale ribbon stretched straight across the sky. Half a mile downstream there were two eruptions and then a third, close together. The first two looked like some giant had thrown a huge basket of flaming golden oranges high in the air. The third was just a balloon of fire enclosed in black smoke above the housetops. The observer didn't bother with his gun sight and indicator for that one. Just reached for his night glasses, took one quick look, picked up his telephone, and said, "Two high explosives and one oil bomb," and named the street where they had fallen.

There was a small fire going off to our left. Suddenly sparks showered up from it as though someone had punched the middle of a huge campfire with a tree trunk. Again the gun sight swung around, the bearing was read, and the report went down the telephone lines, "There is something in high explosives on that fire at 59."

There was peace and quiet inside for twenty minutes. Then a shower of incendiaries came down far in the distance. They didn't fall in a line. It looked like flashes from an electric train on a wet night, only the engineer was drunk and driving his train in circles through the streets. One sight at the middle of the flashes and our observer reported laconically, "Breadbasket at 90—covers a couple of miles." Half an hour later a string of fire bombs fell right beside the Thames. Their white glare was reflected in the black, lazy water near the banks and faded out in midstream where the moon cut a golden swathe broken only by the arches of famous bridges.

We could see little men shoveling those fire bombs into

the river. One burned for a few minutes like a beacon right in the middle of a bridge. Finally those white flames all went out. No one bothers about the white light, it's only when it turns yellow that a real fire has started.

I must have seen well over a hundred fire bombs come down and only three small fires were started. The incendiaries aren't so bad if there is someone there to deal with them, but those oil bombs present more difficulties.

As I watched those white fires flame up and die down, watched the yellow blazes grow dull and disappear, I thought, what a puny effort is this to burn a great city. Finally, we went below to a big room underground. It was quiet. Women spoke softly into telephones. There was a big map of London on the wall. Little colored pins were being moved from one point to another and every time a pin was moved it meant that fire pumps were on their way through the black streets of London to a fire. One district had asked for reinforcements from another, just as an army reinforces its front lines in the sector bearing the brunt of the attack. On another map all the observation posts, like the one I just left, were marked. There was a string with a pin at the end of it dangling from each post position; a circle around each post bore the same markings as I had seen on the tables beneath the gun sight up above. As the reports came in, the string was stretched out over the reported bearing and the pin at the end stuck in the map. Another report came in, and still another, and each time a string was stretched. At one point all those strings crossed and there, checked by a half-dozen cross bearings from different points, was a fire. Watching that system work gave me one of the strangest sensations of the war. For I have seen a similar system used to find the exact location of forest fires out on the Pacific coast.

We picked a fire from the map and drove to it. And the map was right. It was a small fire in a warehouse near the river. Not much of a fire; only ten pumps working on it, but still big enough to be seen from the air. The searchlights were bunched overhead and as we approached we could hear the drone of a German plane and see the burst of anti-aircraft fire directly overhead. Two pieces of shrapnel slapped down in the water and then everything was drowned in the hum of the pumps and the sound of hissing water. Those firemen in their oilskins and tin hats appeared oblivious to everything but the fire. We went to another blaze—just a small two-story house down on the East End. An incendiary had gone through the roof and the place was being gutted. A woman stood on a corner, clutching a rather dirty pillow. A policeman was trying to comfort her. And a fireman said, "You'd be surprised what strange things people pick up when they run out of a burning house."

And back at headquarters I saw a man laboriously and carefully copying names in a big ledger—the list of firemen killed in action during the last month. There were about a hundred names.

I can now appreciate what lies behind those lines in the morning communiqués—all fires were quickly brought under control.

OCTOBER 13, 1940

This is London, one o'clock in the morning, and the moon is almost full, but the heavy cloud rack which scuds

across its face has reduced the moon's value as a bombing
flare. The raid, intense earlier in the evening, seems to be
tapering off now. It started shortly after blackout time. German planes came filtering in singly or in pairs from three
directions. About the usual number of planes are engaged.
A mixture of high explosives and incendiaries has been coming down, but the incendiaries have been doing little damage. There are bombers, not fighters, overhead tonight. No
fighter ever carried the weight of two or three bombs that
have come down tonight.

I spent last night beside my favorite haystack down near
the mouth of the Thames. Things haven't changed much
down there during the last month. The little green and
white pub across the road has suffered a direct hit, but the
countryside is little changed. Apples have been picked and
the hops have been harvested. But last night wasn't like
that night a month ago when we watched that first big attack against London. The siren sounded at the usual time,
but the guns didn't rave and roar as they did. Only a few
planes came over. We could see no fires up the river. Sometime after midnight, as the gray mists crawled over the
fields and rivers, we heard the "all-clear," faint but distinct
in the distance. After that the only noise was produced by
a night owl. Early this morning we drove to Folkestone, a
town that was sad and forlorn on this Sunday forenoon, but
where you still must search to find the damage. Then on to
Dover for lunch. I'd heard many tales of what had happened to Dover during the last few weeks, but the town's
still there. Our favorite hotel has been smashed and a few
more streets have been roped off, but the new damage is
not great. Our lunch consisted of mock-turtle soup (I think

it came out of a can), roast beef and Yorkshire pudding, potatoes, cabbage, something called a pie, cheese, and coffee —and it cost about fifty cents. Not bad for lunch in the front line.

Returning, we visited the old cathedral town of Canterbury, wanted to see what had happened to it after the Germans had announced that it had been one of their principal targets during one of last week's raids. That raid killed five people and knocked down a few buildings. The cathedral still stands. Only a few substitute windows were blown out. The little old wooden houses near by weren't made to stand up to this sort of thing, and some of them, but not many, collapsed. The big cathedral still towers over the plains. This afternoon seven pigeons plowed aimlessly through the dead leaves under the big trees. A New Zealand soldier and his girl strolled about with no more obvious purpose. A lance corporal took a picture of his sergeant standing beside the main entrance. There was an air-raid warning in force. A squadron of British fighters, almost invisible, high in the blue sky, swung in a slow circle above the cathedral. They left a trail behind them in the clear-blue sky, a trail that looked like the wake of fast speedboats on blue-green water. A quarter of a mile behind this squadron, cutting in and out of feathery white wakes, came a single plane, swerving from side to side in slow, graceful sweeps like a surf rider—the lone fighter covering the rear of the fighter patrol.

We came back to London on the other side of the river, the south side near the docks. The damage to small dwellings has been severe. Not all the German bombs hit the docks—and poor people live near those docks. Entire streets are uninhabitable. The sun was still in the sky, but men, women, and children were already flowing toward the shelters, and the shelters down here are none too good.

Somehow the damage wasn't as great as I'd expected, but then it seldom is. One hears stories of whole blocks laid flat, and when you find only three or four houses down and the rest with their windows out, it doesn't seem as bad as you'd expected. One or two general impressions remain after this quick trip along both sides of the Thames and along the southeast coast. The first is that glass is not an ideal building material in this year of disgrace. The second, that high-explosive bombs are not an ideal weapon for the destruction of the human race; something more devastating is required. But many of the best scientific brains of the world are engaged on that problem and presumably they'll find a solution in time.

No one could avoid being impressed with the patience and calm determination of these people who dwell in the little houses. Not all of them can leave London. Indeed, many of them refuse to leave. During the winter months they will face great danger, not only from bombs but from epidemics. Those responsible for home security realize the magnitude of their task, and they're making progress, for they know that upon the success of their efforts all else depends.

OCTOBER 17, 1940

Perhaps you'd like to know what's being advertised in London's newspapers after forty days and forty nights of air raids. Here's a random selection taken from today's papers. On the front page is the old favorite—hair tonic, under the title "*Why be gray? Gray hair makes you look old before your time.*" And here's a product which claims that by its use one lonely egg can be made into scrambled eggs for two. A half-column advertisement headed "*Fly with the Royal Air Force,*" and opposite that a quarter column of type which extols the virtues of something that will clean hands as well as pots, pans, and woodwork. A shoe store strikes a topical note with the picture of a man wearing a pained expression, saying, "*My feet are Fifth Columns.*" There are dozens of advertisements for cough medicines, coffee, shoeshine polish, and preparations for cleaning false teeth. We're told of various remedies for shelter sickness, colds, sore throats, and so forth. An anonymous nurse advises how to cure cross babies. And the whisky distiller says his product is invaluable for any emergency and is a shield against colds and ills and all sorts of chills.

A secondhand automobile dealer is still willing to send a car on trial. A number of organizations are willing to help in filling out income-tax forms. And a certain Mr. Billston says, "*My nerves feel steadier*" after taking a certain kind of nerve tonic. A dockmaster says he was a prisoner in his room for five years, a helpless victim of nerves, but made a magnificent recovery after taking some of the tablets. Of course, long before this war started the British were great purchasers of patent medicines.

A small box in the afternoon paper tells us that there will be greyhound racing at a big sports arena tomorrow. And here's a strange item—a special brand of cocoa, advertised at less than prewar prices. And up in Glasgow *Gone With the Wind* is in its twenty-first week, but must end soon. And, finally, a chain of retail tailors believes its customers have a good chance of surviving the *blitz*. It offers suits on a small down payment with twelve months to pay.

NOVEMBER 11, 1940

I want to tell you something about Cherry Brandy. Of course that isn't his real name—just an irreverent but affectionate title given by some of his friends who have difficulty pronouncing Dutch names. For Cherry Brandy is a little Dutchman. He is, in fact, the number-one Dutchman, Prime Minister of The Netherlands. His whole name is Nikolaas Gerbrandi. He is a little man, considerably less than five feet tall, bald head, twinkling blue eyes, a thoroughly undisciplined walrus mustache which would give any other man a ferocious appearance but seems to be a badge of benign benevolence as worn by Cherry Brandy. He has, too, a stomach which has got a little out of control, but then no one could imagine him without that stomach to support the heavy gold watch chain draped across his front. His Excellency walks through this troubled world on small feet encased in black, square-toed, sensible shoes. Most of the time the cares of the world and the Dutch Empire rest without obvious weight upon his square shoulders. He wears life lightly, like a loose garment. Cherry Brandy is no politician. He became Prime Minister after the Dutch government moved to London. He explained his life's history to me the other day in this fashion, "I was for many years," he said, "a professor of international law at the University of Amsterdam. One day they came to me and said, 'We must have a chairman, a kind of arbitrator for the four Dutch broadcasting companies.' But I said, 'I

don't know anything about broadcasting.' 'That's fine,' they
said. 'You take the job,' and I did. We had some excellent
battles," says Cherry Brandy, "but I became interested in
broadcasting, and the international conferences we had, particularly those in Switzerland, were very nice." He likes
climbing mountains, has all the love of a man who lives on
flat land for the rough, wild country that stands on edge.
Continuing his life story, the Prime Minister said, "Suddenly I became Minister of Justice and then more suddenly
Prime Minister." He is, so far as I know, the first broadcaster ever to become prime minister of any country. I suspect that he is a bad politician. There is no compromise in
his make-up. His ability to silence the bombastic and ver-
bose is unequaled.

A few years ago at a radio conference in Berlin he was
dining with a colleague of mine and with a high Nazi official. The official was explaining in rather grandiose fashion
that he would be delighted to show the foreign broadcasters
any and all of the institutions of modern Germany. They
could, he said, visit the Hitler youth camps, the labor camps
—yes, and even the concentration camps. At that point
Cherry Brandy, with a twinkle in his blue eyes and every
outward appearance of gratitude for this generous offer,
looked the Nazi official straight in the eyes and said with a
smile that was partially concealed by his walrus mustache,
"Visit the concentration camps? That would be very nice,
but I fear to find all my friends there."

Cherry Brandy is a man with great faith, humility, and
even today optimism. He lunched with me in a fashionable
London restaurant the other day. When the waiter brought
the soup he bowed his head for half a minute with the same

unassuming, simple dignity that would have been his had
we been lunching at home with his family in Holland. His
family, by the way, is still in Holland, but he has faith that
they will be all right. About the final outcome of the war
he is optimistic. Exactly how it is to be won is not clear, but
in Cherry Brandy's mind there is no doubt of the outcome.
He simply says, "Under the Nazis there can be no human
life, none, and that cannot be." The Dutch East Indies, he
says, will fight. They can hold out for some time, but in the
end it will all depend on what America does. This little man
is proud of the Indies, proud of his former students who are
out there, and justly proud of the Dutch record of colonial
administration.

You might think that this Prime Minister of a nation
which has only its empire left would revere and respect
some of the empire builders of the past or perhaps the
statesmen of today. But nothing of the kind. His respect
and reverence is for an academic colleague of his who spent
his life teaching Dutch students about colonial administration and convincing them that their university training
placed upon them a great obligation toward those less well
equipped, that it gave them no privileges but rather a duty
to repay a society which had made possible their education.
About two things the Dutch Prime Minister is dogmatic:
that the Dutch have handled their overseas possessions
more wisely and humanely than any other nation and that
Dutch gin taken in moderation is the best drink in the
world. England he likes—particularly the universities, cathe-
drals, and the green fields. Sometimes the fields, those that
are flat, remind him of Holland, and when he is reminded
of Holland he may talk of the privations that the coming

winter will bring to his people, of the homeless in Rotterdam, or of the morning mists that rise and hang above the tulip fields. All that is good and admirable in Holland and the Dutch people is in this short, sturdy little man. All the decency, devotion to duty and democracy, loyalty to family and friends—yes, and all the love of laughter, good food and drink, too. The chancelleries of the world do not hang anxiously upon his words and actions. Radio and the cables do not flash his every word around the world. Here in London, the seat of his government and the refuge of his Queen, not one person out of a thousand could even tell you the name of the Prime Minister of The Netherlands, but true greatness is not measured by such fleeting standards. Cherry Brandy, of course, would be the last to call himself a great man. His sense of humor is too keen for that.

The other night he was standing in a doorway waiting for his car to pick him up. Incidentally, he never possessed a car before he became Prime Minister. There was a terrific barrage going up and shrapnel was clattering down all around. Someone said, "Surely, you're not going out in that, Mr. Prime Minister," and Cherry Brandy replied with a chuckle, "Yes, I go. I think I make a very small target."

NOVEMBER 18, 1940

The other night—it might have been almost any wet night in mid-November—I heard a sound as I stood on a street corner. It was dark—time for the night raid to start. There was no traffic on the street. Big raindrops shattered themselves against the wooden paving blocks. The sound that I heard was caused by the raindrops, but they were not hitting the pavement. It was a crisp, bouncing sound. Some of you have heard that sound as the rain drummed on a tent roof. Three people, old people they were, stood beside me in the rain and murk; they were on their way to the shelters. The bedding rolls were hunched high on their shoulders, and the blankets and pillows were wrapped in oilcloth. And a more chilling, brutal sound is not to be heard in London. As those three people squelched away in the darkness, looking like repugnant humpbacked monsters, I couldn't help thinking after all they're rather lucky—there are hundreds of thousands who haven't even oilcloth to wrap their bedding rolls.

Sounds, as well as words, get all twisted in wartime. Familiar harmless sounds take on a sinister meaning. And, for me, the sound of raindrops hitting windowpanes, tar roofs, or tents will always bring back those three misshapen people on a London street corner on a wet November night.

NOVEMBER 27, 1940

I should like to tell you about a completely unimportant incident that occurred in a small village I know down in Essex. A thin man, wearing a big, loose overcoat and a black hat with the brim brushed down till it nearly hit his right eye, walked into the bar of a public house. In a husky voice he asked for dry sherry. Sitting down in a fire-shadowed corner he took out a notebook and began to write with the stub of a pencil. The regular customers, standing near the dart's board looked him over carefully and in whispers urged one of their number to make contact with the mysterious stranger. And so ignoring the big clock over the bar, one of the locals went over and asked for the time, and he also tried to see what the stranger was writing. The stranger exhibited a watch and the local couldn't make anything of the strange scrawls and convolutions on the notebook. "Is that the right time?" he said. "Yah," replied the man in the black hat. Back at the dart's board there were whispers of "German" and "spy." One member of the team eased out into the dusk in search of a policeman. When he returned with a tin-hatted representative of the law, the stranger was engaged in a game of darts with two members of the local home guard. The policeman come in, viewed the situation, and, being by nature cautious, did not arrest the suspicious stranger immediately. For he was no Fifth Columnist, just a reporter; the "yah" was the American monosyllable "yeah," and the strange hieroglyphics on the notebook, believed to be code, turned out to be nothing but shorthand.

NOVEMBER 29, 1940

Yesterday the American correspondents in London had a session with the Minister of Information. We talked mainly about censorship. After more than a year of practice, the system remains unpredictable and erratic. It is still the most liberal system of censorship in Europe, but sometimes, in an effort to mislead Britain's enemies, it succeeds only in misleading or confusing her friends. Mr. Duff Cooper made it quite clear that he would rather sacrifice a good headline than risk revealing information to the enemy. And the American correspondents left him in no doubt as to their objection to the operation of his censorship department.

I have no desire to defend any system of censorship, but you should know that you're receiving in general more information than the British public, concerning the progress of this war. It is, of course, true that German bombs hit things other than churches and hospitals, but it is unreasonable to expect the British to confirm the success of German bombing of military and industrial objectives. And whether it's reasonable or not, they aren't going to do it. The expression of opinion is still free in this country: material is published in the daily press and in news letters which would cause the author to lose his head in any other belligerent nation.

You have been told that Britain faces the darkest days since Dunkerque, and it's true that the figures of shipping losses are ominous; but a substantially greater number of aircraft were produced in October than in September. And confidential reports submitted to the government, not for publication, indicate that civilian morale is higher now than it was last week or at this time last month.

DECEMBER 1, 1940

There is occurring a certain change in the temper of the House of Commons. Last week in the debates covering the question of man power and production one had the feeling that Mr. Churchill had lost but little of his hold over the House. At the same time it was clear that many members felt that the able and brilliant commander in chief had not surrounded himself with ministers willing to take the drastic steps necessary to reorganize the economy of the country.

There is a fairly widespread demand that the government's compulsory powers be more fully used.* The training of skilled workers and the slowness with which women have been introduced into industry were severely criticized. So far as the people of this country are concerned, there is every reason to believe that they would welcome a wider and speedier use of the government's compulsory powers. There is widespread realization that the breaking of Germany's counterblockade is the most urgent of many problems and that it can only be done by increased production.

There are still more people willing, anxious, and asking what they can do than there are those who complain that too much is being asked of them. Lord Lothian's calculated indiscretion in mentioning the eventual need for American money is still being discussed. The general impression in London is that when the time comes, the money will be provided. Some argue that American plants expanded by British orders would be forced to close when present assets are absorbed, and it would be cheaper for the government to provide credits to keep them open. Others say more bluntly: "The Americans say this is their war that we're fighting. If we're going to fight it, they ought to help pay for it."

Considerable surprise has been expressed over the amount of looting in bombing areas. It hasn't reached large-scale proportions, but the British are always surprised at any increase in lawlessness. The matter is further complicated by the fact that many of the articles picked up from the bombed houses are of little intrinsic value, a book or a

---

* But not till the end of January, 1941, was this demand so urgent that the government actually began seriously to threaten to use them.

piece of ribbon or a bucketful of coal, that sort of thing. Many people convicted of looting are certainly not criminal types and have not taken the objects for reasons of personal gain. One has a strange feeling, or at least I have, in looking at the contents of a bombed house or shop that the things scattered about don't belong to anyone. It's as though they, together with the bomb, had just dropped out of the sky. Picking up a book or a pipe that's been blown into the street is almost like picking an apple in a deserted and over-grown orchard far from any road or house.

DECEMBER 2, 1940

These broadcasts are done from London at a quarter to one in the morning. Sometimes when they're ended, there is no desire to sleep, only the urge to go out and walk familiar streets at a time when the night is left to darkness and to me. Wandering around the streets of this city in the early hours of the morning is sometimes exciting; there may be fires, gunfire, and bombs. One may see in the light of flares, scarcely hidden under canvas, human beings, looking like broken, cast-away, dust-covered barrels, being lifted with careful hands out of a tunnel driven through to the basement of a bombed house. But more often the streets are empty, the guns silent, and one walks the streets of this proud city accompanied only by a rabble of undisciplined random thoughts. The sight of a familiar church spire reminds one of Churchill's remarks that it will take ten years to destroy half the city, and that after that progress will be slower. Or of Duff Cooper's comment that most of Europe, if not the world, will be destroyed in this war.

Occasionally during November and December a cold, choking fog comes down to take command of the streets; it seeps down into the shelters and the subways. After a visit to one of those shelters, one climbs the stairs into the damp darkness of the night, pursued by the sound of coughing and hoping that it will be a mild winter in Europe. During a heavy raid, courage varies in direct proportion to the cold. It's difficult to be brave when you're cold. Sometimes looking in at a fashionable hotel with its bright lights, music, and champagne, and the empty, unfeeling faces of the dancers on the floor, we're reminded again of the Prime Minister's phrase: grim and gay. Those people are neither grim nor gay. One must go to the subways and see men playing poker for a twopenny limit, women brewing tea, or cab drivers talking on the ranks, to understand that phrase. There are times, too, when thoughts of English writers who have sought refuge in the States recur. For them there can be only sympathy. No matter how able they may be, they will have no language and no words to move or impress those who have lived through this.

Stumbling through the darkness, you're inclined to think of shipping losses—about 60,000 tons a week since June— and to wonder how many ships of medium size that represents. There is time, too, to think of British courtesy as well as courage, the good-humored courtesy of taxi drivers and bus conductors, of people who still thank you for asking them to do you a favor, even when it's hard to hear their thanks above the roar of the guns. One night during a terrific barrage I saw a little man wearing a tin hat, running down the middle of the street. He tripped over a rope stretched across the street to prevent traffic from passing.

His tin hat rolled into the gutter. He retrieved it and said to no one at all—he was quite alone in the street—"Sorry, so sorry," and then he went on his way. Those of us who have been trying to report this war have said too much about courage and too little about courtesy. People who remember to be courteous are not greatly afraid.

Walking from Regent Park to the Embankment there is time to think of the frequent comments overheard during the day—Londoners saying they wish it had been London instead of Liverpool or Southampton that was bombed last night. They know the value of their ports, but it's interesting that they would rather have had the bombs aimed at them than at more vital points. In the early hours of the morning, sometime between five and seven, the high, steady note of the "all-clear" cuts through the cold, frosty air of London. Hundreds of thousands of humans come oozing up from underground, many of them stiff and tired from a night in the shelter. The ducks in Green Park set up their questioning quacking and the pigeons come back from some mysterious place to Trafalgar Square. Buckets of boiling water are poured into the muzzles of hard-worked guns, as they are swabbed out and prepared for another night's work. And always as one walks home with the winter's sun boring through the autumn mist there is the question: How long can this go on?

DECEMBER 3, 1940

A theory advanced by certain British and American journalists in the weeks preceding the American presidential election has perished. That theory was that the United

States would be of greater help to Britain as a nonbelligerent than as a full-fledged ally. The British, in spite of surface impartiality, wanted President Roosevelt to win the
election. They encouraged this theory that American assistance, based on peacetime organization, would be more effective than full-scale belligerent aid. It had the advantage
of reassuring those American voters who feared that the
country might be involved in a war. Since the election, we
have heard nothing of this thesis. It's a dead and dynamited
fish, and you would have difficulty in finding any responsible British official with a desire to revive it. It's possible
that for a time certain Britishers believed that American aid
on a neutral basis would be adequate and effective. If they
thought so, their disillusionment has been rapid. Ask any
member of Parliament or any member of the government
whether he prefers a neutral America or a belligerent America, and you will get only one answer. Some would express
a preference for winning the war without American aid, but
most would admit that it can't be done.

I'm reporting what I believe to be the dominant informed
opinion in this country. Later on, you may hear it expressed
by responsible British spokesmen. There are no indications
that any British minister is going to urge you to declare war
against the Axis, but you must expect repeated references in
the press and in public statements to the British belief that
a democratic nation at peace cannot render full and effective support to a nation at war, for that is what the majority
of thinking people in this country have come to believe. As
a reporter I'm concerned to report this development not to
evaluate it in terms of personal approval or disapproval.

DECEMBER 5, 1940

The House of Commons devoted considerable time today to debating peace aims. The Independent Labour party introduced a motion urging the government to state its aims and terms for ending this conflict. Mr. Attlee, leader of the Labour party, replying for the government, termed it an irresponsible motion and said that a further statement of British aims would be made at a suitable time. Mr. Churchill used that phrase some time ago, and, when asked what he meant by a suitable time, replied: "A time that is suitable." Mr. Attlee believed that there was general understanding of British war aims, and he said: "We are trying to establish a world of peace under a free people." The four members of the Independent Labour party voted for their motion; 341 members voted against. The debate will be characterized as a waste of time in a world where the strong exact what they can and the weak suffer what they must.

It had been believed that Mr. Churchill might take the opportunity to make a more definite statement of British war aims, but he took no part in the debate. The opinion is still held in the highest quarters here that no adequate definition of democracy's objectives can be made until it comes from Washington, or in a joint declaration from Washington and London and that presupposes American entry into the war. There's another school of thought which says that the British must be sure in their own minds and be able to convince the Americans that the new world order which America is asked to join in making is not merely a device to maintain the *status* quo for the benefit of the British Commonwealth.

I'd like to read you a large poster which is headed: FOR
WHAT ARE BRITAINS AT WAR? "For the undisturbed exercise
of their religion; for the preservation of their government
and laws; for the maintenance of their personal liberties;
for the protection of their families and friends; for the continuation of their trade and commerce; for the enjoyment
of their property and wealth; for the security of their lives
and political existence; for the vindication of their national
honor; for the revival and extension of European freedom,
and for the restoration of peace and happiness to man."

The program issued for review of the volunteer corps in
Hyde Park contained the phrase: "Burdens and privations
are submitted to with cheerfulness, because we're convinced
of their necessity." A dictator bent on invasion of England
when asked, "What do you most depend on for your success?" replied: "On foggy weather, long nights, a want of
discipline in your troops, a want of spirit and union in your
people." A member of Parliament, William Wilberforce,
declared: "We bear upon us but too plainly the marks of a
declining empire." He urged the faithful to pray in the
hope that God might for a while avert our ruin. He said that
to the decline of religion and morality our national difficulties must both directly and indirectly be chiefly ascribed.
Mr. Wilberforce was re-elected member of Parliament for
Yorkshire in the year 1802. Napoleon was the man determined to invade England, and it was in 1803 when his
armies were massed on the French Channel that that poster
of war aims, more definite and precise than anything we've
had in 1940, was plastered on the walls of towns and villages throughout England.

I've told you of the reply given by Mr. Attlee in today's

question in the House of Commons on the subject of war aims or, rather, peace aims. Probably the simplest and certainly the briefest statement of war aims ever made must be attributed to Jan Masaryk, the exiled Foreign Minister of the Czechoslovakian government now in London. He said: "I want to go home."

DECEMBER 23, 1940

This afternoon I followed my steaming breath down Regent Street. It was cold, plenty of fur coats and heavy tweeds being worn. A few soldiers on leave wearing their Balaklava helmets, but there was a tough-looking Canadian sergeant striding along without so much as an overcoat. A couple of Australian privates stood near Oxford Circus having a grand time, snapping to attention and saluting everytime a new second lieutenant came along with his arms loaded with packages. There were a few families doing last-minute shopping, the children asking to be lifted up so they could see through the small panes of glass surrounded by cardboard, the only display space of stores that formerly presented their goods behind acres of plate glass. Taxi drivers waiting in the ranks flinging their arms to keep warm. Two RAF trucks were drawn up in front of one big store. One corporal, who spoke with the slow drawl of a west countryman, said: "The commanding officer's a fine bloke to buy all these presents for the station, but I'd like to see a few barrels of beer in all this lot."

In the entire curving length of that famous street, I saw not a single Christmas tree. I could see no decorations of any kind, but the windows were full of practical presents.

In Piccadilly Circus, men were placing new sandbags and boards around the statue of Eros; wandering down toward Trafalgar Square I found more men working on a week-old bomb crater. Against the fading and uncertain light of winter dusk, I could see Lord Nelson standing atop his column in the center of the Square.

Walking home through streets rapidly being drained of life and movement, I heard the sirens announcing the night raid. As that warning wail crept through the winter night, I thought of the Englishmen and women from Charing Cross to China who would be thinking of London on the night before Christmas Eve and decided to try to tell them about it. The only thing I can add to what I've said is that I saw no smiling, merry faces, nor did I see any signs of gloom or despair—only the calm, placid expression one sees on Londoners' faces when they're waiting for a bus.

One thing more—on the way home I heard Christmas carols twice. The singing was steady and firm and it came from underground. And tonight's raid opened early. The gunfire had been fairly heavy and the German planes have been over the city since darkness fell, but it has not been a heavy night.

DECEMBER 24, 1940

This is London, reporting all clear. There was a single German aircraft over East Anglia this afternoon, but there are no reports of German raiders over Britain tonight. Whether this inactivity is due to good will or bad weather, I don't know, nor do we know whether the RAF bombers are flying tonight. Christmas Day began in London nearly

an hour ago. The church bells did not ring at midnight.
When they ring again, it will be to announce invasion. And
if they ring, the British are ready. Tonight, as on every other
night, the rooftop watchers are peering out across the fantastic forest of London's chimney pots. The antiaircraft
gunners stand ready. And all along the coast of this island,
the observers revolve in their reclining chairs, listening for
the sound of German planes. The fire fighters and the ambulance drivers are waiting, too. The blackout stretches
from Birmingham to Bethlehem, but tonight over Britain
the skies are clear.

This is not a merry Christmas in London. I heard that
phrase only twice in the last three days. This afternoon as
the stores were closing, as shoppers and office workers were
hurrying home, one heard such phrases as "So long,
Mamie," and "Good luck, Jack," but never "A merry
Christmas." It can't be a merry Christmas, for those people
who spend tonight and tomorrow by their firesides in their
own homes realize that they have bought this Christmas
with their nerves, their bodies, and their old buildings. Their
nerve is unshaken; the casualties have not been large, and
there are many old buildings still untouched. Between now
and next Christmas there stretches twelve months of increasing toil and sacrifice, a period when the Britishers will
live hard. Most of them realize that. Tonight's serious
Christmas Eve is the result of a realization of the future,
rather than the aftermath of hardships sustained during the
past year. The British find some basis for confidence in the
last few months' developments. They believe that they're
tearing the Italian Empire to pieces. So far shelter life has

produced none of the predicted epidemics. The nation's health is about as good now as it was at this time last year. And above all they're sustained by a tradition of victory.

Tonight there are few Christmas parties in London, a few expensive dinners at famous hotels, but there are no fancy paper hats and no firecrackers. Groups determined to get away from the war found themselves after twenty minutes inspecting the latest amateur diagram of the submarine menace or the night bombers. A few blocks away in the underground shelters entire families were celebrating Christmas Eve. Christmas carols are being sung underground. Most of the people down there don't know that London is not being bombed tonight. Christmas presents will be unwrapped down underground before those people see daylight tomorrow. Little boys who have received miniature Spitfires or Hurricanes will be waking the late sleepers by imitating the sound of whistling bombs, just as we used to try to reproduce the sound of a locomotive or a speeding automobile.

So far as tonight's news is concerned, we're told that Herr Hess, Hitler's deputy, has offered a prayer, and has asked God to assist Hitler to fight and to work for our eternal wonderful Germany, so that Germany shall continue to be worthy of God's blessings. We are told, too, that on the occasion of Christmas the King of Italy has sent a message to his fighting forces in which he says that his grateful thoughts are with them—no obstacles can stop the glorious ascent of Italy. King Victor Emmanuel is confident of a radiant future.

I should like to add my small voice to give my own Christmas greetings to friends and colleagues at home. Merry Christmas is somehow ill-timed and out of place, so I shall just use the current London phrase—so long and good luck.

DECEMBER 29, 1940

(Part of a year-end summary by various speakers)

The first year of the famished forties is ending. All Europe is on short rations. It was Hitler's year. The record of the last twelve months stretches endlessly back over blasted hopes, futile ambitions, false confidence, small men, and a wreckage of proud and pleasant nations. For those of us who have lived in Britain it has been a long year. Many of its memories have been blasted away by bombs or lost in the whirlwind of events. Last year at this time people in London were calling it a "bore war," singing songs about hanging out the washing on the Siegfried Line—the small British Army in France was being reinforced; we were told that time was on the side of the Allies; that the Navy's ring of steel would gradually squeeze Germany to death; Mr. Chamberlain was Prime Minister; the Finns were fighting the Russians, and the British were sending them ambulances, fire engines, and field kitchens, even as America is now sending similar gear to Britain. RAF planes flying from advance bases in France were dropping leaflets on Germany. The cold months of January and February passed, the British government was almost in hibernation—a twilight sleep of overconfidence. On the thirteenth of March the Finns signed a treaty in Moscow and the unequal struggle was ended. Certain sections of British opinion became restive,

wanted to know why more had not been done to help the
Finns. There was a Cabinet reshuffle, nothing more than a
changing of labels.

The number of registered unemployed, after six months
of war, was still well above the million mark. Mr. Chamberlain, on April 4, was ten times as confident of victory as he
was at the beginning. Hitler had missed the bus. Four days
later the British and French vessels planted mines in Norwegian territorial waters. The following day Germany in-
vaded Denmark and Norway. Six days later the first British
troops, ill-equipped, ill-trained, landed in Norway. Some of
the officers had their fishing rods with them. British spokesmen asserted that Hitler had made a major strategic error.
Fantastic reports, claiming the recapture of Bergen and
Trondheim, were published and broadcast. It was claimed
that the Norwegian counteroffensive was developing satisfactorily. There were naval engagements between light
forces in the Skagerrak and the British sank seven German
destroyers in Narvik Bay. On April 26, the War Office admitted a slight withdrawal south of Dombaas. The German
advance toward Trondheim was unexpectedly rapid. On the
second of May came the news that Allied troops had withdrawn from Aandalsnes. The following day, British and
French forces were brought off from Namsos. Fighting
around Narvik continued but the Norwegian campaign was
ended.

Then came a two-day post-mortem in the House of Commons—two days and nights of drama and bitterness—
Churchill, attempting to defend his chief, Neville Chamberlain; Admiral of the Fleet, Sir Roger Keyes, telling how
he begged permission to use old warships to force an en-

trance into Trondheim; David Lloyd George, brushing back his long white hair before lashing Chamberlain with words of scorn in that musical Welsh voice. Jeers and insults flew like shrapnel across that room and, at the end of it all, Neville Chamberlain walked out alone, a beaten, broken man.

Two days later the German armies poured into the Low Countries and on that same day Winston Churchill, an Englishman of note, became Prime Minister of Great Britain. He reorganized the government, secured the co-operation of the Labour party, and since that time this combination of scholar, statesman, and eighteenth-century cavalry officer has dominated wartime Britain. His appointment as Prime Minister may have been the most important event in 1940.

The British watched the German scythe cut through Holland, Belgium, and northern France with a dazed feeling of unbelief. The Channel ports were lost; the Belgians capitulated. We were told that the British and French were falling back on Dunkerque—a name that will live as long as the English language. The British Expeditionary Force appeared lost, but an armada was formed—surely the strongest ever assembled. It was made up of pleasure yachts, motorboats, trawlers, paddle steamers, skippered by men without fear of salt water or German bombs, and they went across to Dunkerque, eight hundred and eighty-seven vessels, and brought their boys back. I saw them arrive. Many of them were dazed, battered, and bleeding, but they were not beaten. Their equipment had been lost.

Men and women worked in factories as they had never worked before to replace it.

When France asked for an armistice on June 17, the average Britisher did not realize the enormity of the disaster that had befallen Britain. She never had a very high regard for foreigners, anyway. On June 10, a day when the air in London was heavy and lifeless, Mussolini declared war and the British were still undismayed. They worked feverishly on their coast defenses, determined to justify Churchill's prediction that they would fight on the beaches, in the streets, and on the hills. The summer weather was kind, the crops were good, the Germans did some fairly heavy bombing during the day and night. In August the tempo of the air war increased. The Germans were hammering fighter dromes along the coast. At first, the British fought them over Dover in the Channel, then over Kent and, finally, over London. On the fifteenth of August, the Germans lost a hundred and eighty planes but still they kept coming. Late in the afternoon of September 7, German bombers flying in tight formation came roaring up over the Thames Estuary. All afternoon and all night they bombed the docks and East End of London—four hundred people killed, thousands injured, and huge red fires lighting the night sky as London burned. For ten days we were bombed day and night but the invaders didn't come. Civilian casualties were less than had been anticipated. The Germans switched to night bombing and have been at it ever since. No one expects them to stop—in fact, we're being bombed again tonight, and very heavily, too.

As 1940 ends, Britain is in mortal danger. The only good news is that from the western desert and it is recognized that those operations are of secondary importance. No one expects the new year to be happy. We shall live hard before it is ended. The immediate problems are many and varied. Something must be done about the night bomber and the submarines; improved facilities for life underground must be provided, and the supply of material from overseas must continue. A year ago today you would have found few people in Britain willing to admit that American action would determine the outcome of this war, but today the realization is widespread—the decisions taken in Washington will determine the course of this war during the coming year or years. Britishers have seen a powerful enemy advance almost to their very homes and fail to dare invasion. They've seen the beginning of great social changes and have faced death in the streets and by their firesides. They have been grim and gay, true to their traditions, and they will not act otherwise in 1941. Probably the best summary of this year that is dying was written by Wordsworth in 1806: "Another year, another deadly blow, another mighty empire overthrown, and we are left or shall be left alone—the last that dared to struggle with the foe."

DECEMBER 31, 1940

This is London! The new year is nearly an hour old and we have not been bombed tonight. There are a few crowds in the center of London and a few people in the subways are wearing paper hats, but in general the streets are dark and rather silent. Occasionally there is the sound of riotous singing or a plaintive voice shouting for a taxi, the sound of a phonograph, clinking glasses, and laughing voices filter out through a closely shuttered window. The big red busses that roam the streets are nearly empty. Earlier the pubs

were full. Not much drunkenness but plenty of laughter
and high spirits. The stakes in the dart game were up to ten
cents a game instead of the usual nickel. Men clustered
about the halfpenny board and cheered a good shot. At
one of the pubs a little man wearing a cap and a violent red
tie was trying to tell how he once shot rabbits from a motor-
boat. I never did discover how he achieved that remarkable
feat, for his skeptical audience wouldn't let him finish the
story. An elderly shapeless woman, wearing a faded red vel-
vet coat with a bedraggled rabbit fur collar, fumbled in her
purse to see if she had enough coppers left for another glass
of port. I visited a few air-raid shelters. They were only
about half full. In one, a small baby was squalling; in another, seven men were rehearsing a play they were putting
on for the children. The only inhabitant of a damp, brick-
surface shelter was an inhospitable old gray tabby cat that
spat at me when I showed my flashlight inside.

The fashionable hotels are crowded. They are singing
Auld Lang Syne. I'm told on good authority that the evening dresses are smart and expensive. The exiles in London,
the Poles, Czechs, Dutch, and all the rest are having their
own parties. The Scotsmen who can get away from London
have gone north of the border to celebrate Hogmanay
Night in the traditional fashion.

This is the night when each man's thoughts are his own.
On the surface there are many signs of cheerfulness and
courage in London tonight. There is no regretting the year
that is dead and little prophecy about the year that begins.
Britain has been hit hard and cruelly—will be again—but she
still stands where she did. One slogan for the new year,
given by Herbert Morrison, the Home Secretary, tonight is:

"Fall in, the fire fighters!" Every factory, shop, and private dwelling is to be under observation during air raids. The fires in Manchester, London, and other cities would have caused much less damage had a full-scale system of watchers been in force. Speed is all important in handling incendiaries and within the next few weeks there will be hundreds of thousands of Britishers standing by with hand pumps and buckets of sand whenever the sirens wail at night.

The campaign to grow more foods this year has already started. The slogan for those who take up allotments of public ground or who have gardens of their own is: "Better backache than heartache."

Most of you are probably preparing to welcome the new year. May you have a pleasant evening. You will have no dawn raid as we shall probably have if the weather is right. You may walk this night in the light. Your families are not scattered by the winds of war. You may drive your high-powered car as far as time and money will permit. Only those who have been undernourished for years are in danger of going hungry. You have not been promised blood and toil and tears and sweat and, yet, it is the opinion of nearly every informed observer over here that the decisions you take will overshadow all else during this year that opened an hour ago in London.

During this last year we have tried to bring you news and atmosphere without evaluating it in terms of personal approval or disapproval. We've not always succeeded but we've done our best and have done it without dictation or direction from either side of the Atlantic. We shall keep on trying.

SPRING, 1941

[As the final proofs of this book were being sent to the printer, the Columbia Broadcasting System asked Mr. Murrow to devote one of his Sunday-afternoon broadcasts to giving a general impression of England just before the German spring offensive of 1941 was expected to begin. His talk was transcribed in New York and the complete text follows.]

MARCH 9, 1941

Soon it will be spring in England. Already there are flowers in the park, although the parks aren't quite as well kept as they were this time last year. But there's good fighting weather ahead. In four days' time the moon will be full again and there's a feeling in the air that big things will happen soon.

The winter that is ending has been hard, but Londoners have many reasons for satisfaction. There have been no serious epidemics. The casualties from air bombardments have been less than expected. And London meets this spring with as much courage, though less complacency, than at this time last year.

Many ancient buildings have been destroyed. Acts of individual heroism have been commonplace. More damage has been done by fire than by high explosives. The things cast down by the Germans out of the night skies have made hundreds of thousands of people homeless. I've seen them standing cruel cold of a winter morning with tears frozen on their faces looking at the little pile of rubble that was their homes and saying over and over again in a toneless unbelieving way, "What have we done to deserve this?"

But the winter has brought some improved conditions in the underground shelters. It has brought, too, reduced rations; repeated warnings of the imminence of invasion; shorter restrictions upon the freedom of the individual and organizations.

When spring last came to England the country was drifting and almost dozing through a war that seemed fairly remote. Not much had been done to give man power and machinery to the demands of modern war. The story of the spring, summer, and fall is well known to all of you. For the British it was a record of one disaster after another—until those warm, cloudless days of August and September when the young men of the Royal Air Force beat back the greatest air fleet ever assembled by any nation. Those were the days and nights and even weeks when time seemed to stand still. At the beginning they fought over the English Channel, then over the coast of Kent, and when the German bombers smashed the advance fighter bases along the coast the battle moved inland. Night after night the obscene glare of hundreds of fires reddened the bellies of the big, awkward barrage balloons over London, transforming them into queer animals with grace and beauty. Finally the threat was beaten off. Both sides settled down to delivering heavy blows in the dark. Britain received more than she gave. All through the winter it went on. Finally there came bits of good news from the western desert. But even Tobruk and Bengazi seemed far away. Victories over the Italians are taken for granted here. Even the children know that the real enemy is Germany.

It hasn't been victories in the Middle East or promises of American aid that have sustained the people of this island during the winter. They know that next winter, when it comes, it will probably be worse, that their sufferings and privations will increase. Their greatest strength has been and is something that is talked about a great deal in Germany but never mentioned here—the concept of a master race.

The average Englishman thinks it's just plain silly for the Germans to talk about a master race. He's quietly sure in his own mind that there is only one master race. That's a characteristic that caused him to adopt an attitude of rather bored tolerance toward all foreigners and made him thoroughly disliked by many of them. But it's the thing that has closed his mind to the possibilities that Britain may be defeated.

The habit of victory is strong here. Other habits are strong, too. The old way of doing things is considered best. That's why it has taken more than a year and a half to mobilize Britain's potential strength and the job is not yet finished.

The other day, watching a farmer trying to fill in a twenty-foot-deep bomb crater in the middle of his field, I wondered what would happen before he harvested the next crop from that bomb-torn soil. I suppose that many more bombs will fall. There will be much talk about equality of sacrifice which doesn't exist. Many proud ships will perish in the western approaches. There will be further restrictions on clothes and food. Probably a few profiteers will make their profits.

No one knows whether invasion will come, but there are those who fear it will not. I believe that a public-opinion poll on the question "Would you like the Germans to attempt an invasion?" would be answered overwhelmingly in the affirmative. Most people, believing that it must be attempted eventually, would be willing to have it come soon. They think that in no other way can the Germans win this war, and they will not change their minds until they hear their children say, "We are hungry."

So long as Winston Churchill is Prime Minister, the House of Commons will be given an opportunity to defend its traditions and to determine the character of the government that is to rule this country. The Prime Minister will continue to be criticized in private for being too much interested in strategy and too little concerned with the great social and economic problems that clamor for solution.

British propaganda aimed at occupied countries will continue to fight without its heavy artillery, until some sort of statement on war aims or, if you prefer, peace aims has been published.

And in the future, as in the past, one of the strangest sensations for me will be that produced by radio. Sometime someone will write the story of the technical and military uses to which this new weapon has been put; but no one, I think, will ever describe adequately just what it feels like to sit in London with German bombs ripping in the air, shaking the buildings, and causing the lights to flicker, while you listen to the German radio broadcasting Wagner or Bavarian folk music. A twist of the dial gives you Tokyo talking about dangerous thoughts; an American Senator discussing hemisphere defense; the clipped, precise accent of a British announcer describing the proper method of photographing elephants; Moscow boasting of the prospects of the wheat harvest in the Ukraine; each nation speaking almost any language save its own, until, finally, you switch off the receiving set in order that the sounds from the four corners of the earth will not interfere with the sound of the German bombs that come close enough to cause you to dive under the desk.

The bombs this spring will be bigger and there'll be more of them, probably dropped from a greater height than ever before. Berlin and London will continue to claim that their bombs hit the military targets while the enemy's strike mainly churches, schools, hospitals, and private dwellings.

The opening engagament of the spring campaign is now being fought in the Atlantic. The Admiralty has taken over control of the shipyards in an effort to speed up production and repairs. Merchant sinkings will probably reach alarming proportions, but there will always be men to take ships out. The outcome of the battle in the Atlantic will be decisive. This island lives by its ships, and the ships will be carrying supplies from America.

There was no dancing in the streets here when the "lend-lease" bill was passed, for the British know from their own experience that the gap between legislation and realization can be very wide. They remember being told that their frontier was on the Rhine, and they know now that their government did very little to keep it there.

The course of Anglo-American relations will be smooth on the surface, but many people over here will express regret because they believe America is making the same mistakes that Britain made. For you must understand that the idea of America being of more help as a nonbelligerent than as a fighting ally has been discarded, even by those who advanced it originally. Maybe we shall do some frank, forthright talk across the Atlantic instead of rhetoric, but I doubt it. One thing that is not to be doubted is that the decisions taken in Washington between now and the time the crops are harvested will determine the pattern of events for a long time to come. British statesmen are fond of repeating that Britain stands alone as the defender of democracy and decency, but General Headquarters is now on Pennsylvania Avenue in Washington, D. C. Many Britishers realize that. Not all of them are happy about it, for the policies of Washington have not always been the policies of the Tory party, which still rules this country. Presumably, the decisions of Washington will be taken in the full light of publicity and debate, and no mere radio reporter has the right to use the weight of monopolized opportunity in an effort to influence those decisions. We can only deliver to you an occasional wheelbarrowload of stuff, tell you where it comes from, and what sort of air-raid shelter or bastion you build with it is a matter for free men to decide, but since part of reporting must necessarily be personal, I'd like to end this with my own impression of Britain on the verge of spring and big events.

There's still a sense of humor in the country; the old feeling of superiority over all other peoples remains. So does class distinction. There is great courage and a blind belief that Britain will survive. The British aren't all heroes; they know the feeling of fear; I've shared it with them. They try to avoid thinking deeply about political and social problems. They'll stand any amount of government inefficiency and muddle. They're slow to anger, and they die with great dignity. They will cheer Winston Churchill when he walks through block after block of smashed houses and offices as though he'd brought them a great victory. During a blinding raid when the streets are filled with smoke and the sound of the roaring guns, they'll say to you: "Do you think we're really brave, or just lacking in imagination?"

Well, they've come through the winter, and they've been warned that the testing days are ahead. Of the past months, they may well say: "We've lived a life, not an apology." And of the future, I think most of them would say: "We shall live hard, but we shall live."

EDWARD R. MURROW was born in Greensboro, North Carolina, and was graduated from Washington State College in 1930. He went on to become one of the greatest American journalists of the century, working as director of all foreign offices, as war correspondent, and eventually as European director of CBS. He died in 1965.

WITNESSES TO WAR
FROM SCHOCKEN BOOKS

LIVING THROUGH THE BLITZ
Tom Harrisson, 0-8052-0892-5, paper

"As near an objective history of people at war as we are ever likely to get."
—*Times Literary Supplement*

THIS IS LONDON
Edward R. Murrow, 0-8052-0882-8, paper

"This book is in the full sense the stuff of history—not only to be read now but to be kept for rereading later." —*New York Times*

ORWELL: THE WAR COMMENTARIES
W. J. West, ed., 0-8052-0889-5, paper

"The clarity, the care with which Orwell expresses every nuance, and the tone of evident common sense, are masterful." —*Library Journal*

INTO THE VALLEY
John Hersey, 0-8052-4078-0, hardcover

A minor classic of war reporting by the Pulitzer Prize–winning author of *Hiroshima*.

"A terse, faithful, moving narrative good enough to remind you of Stephen Crane."
—*New Yorker*

MOLLIE & OTHER WAR PIECES
A. J. Liebling, 0-8052-20957-3, paper

An eloquent and engaging collection of Liebling's classic war writings from the *New Yorker*.

THE RED ORCHESTRA
Gilles Perrault, 0-8052-0952-2, paper

"One of the best pieces of reportage on an espionage network to appear in a very long time." —*New York Times Book Review*

OTHER SCHOCKEN AND PANTHEON
TITLES OF INTEREST

NEW YORKER BOOK OF WAR PIECES

Schocken, 0-8052-0901-8, paper; 0-8052-4049-7, cloth

Perhaps the most distinguished collection of World War II journalism ever compiled.
—Just published

THE GOOD WAR

Studs Terkel, Pantheon, 0-394-53103-5, FPT

"Tremendously exciting and very illuminating . . . It will give historians a lot to write about. And for the general reader it will be a revelation." —William L. Shirer

TOTAL WAR

Peter Calvocoressi, Guy Wint, John Pritchard, Pantheon, 0-394-57811-2, cloth

"Remarkable for its enormous wealth of information, its organizational clarity, and the spare simplicity of the writing." *Just published.* *—Publishers Weekly*

IN HITLER'S SHADOW

Richard J. Evans, Pantheon, 0-679-72348-X, paper; 0-394-57686-1, cloth

A brilliant critique of recent attempts by some West German historians to reinterpret and distort the history of the Nazi past. *—Just published*

NAZI GERMANY

IN HITLER'S GERMANY

Bernt Engelmann, Schocken, 0-8052-0864-X, paper

"It conveys the everyday climate of life in the darkest of times. It is a valuable and absorbing addition to the history of the period." *—New York Times Book Review*

FACES OF THE 3RD REICH

Joachim Fest, Pantheon, 0-394-73407-6, paper

"Fest has pulled together in a single volume more details of the lives of his subjects than are included in any other book I can think of."
—Christopher Lehmann-Haupt, *New York Times*

CRISIS OF GERMAN IDEOLOGY

George Mosse, Schocken, 0-8052-0669-8, paper

"A milestone in the study of National Socialism." *—New York Review of Books*

NAZI CULTURE

George Mosse, Schocken, 0-8052-0668-X, paper

"A full picture of the scope and methods of the anticultural vandalism of the Nazis."
—*Christian Science Monitor*

THE WAR IN THE PACIFIC

BY THE BOMB'S EARLY LIGHT

Paul Boyer, Pantheon, 0-394-74767-4, paper

"A pathbreaking study . . . the first to document in detail just how the bomb figured in the nation's public discourse and popular mythology between 1945 and 1950 . . ."
—*Newsweek*

WAR WITHOUT MERCY

John Dower, Pantheon, 0-394-75172-8, paper

"May well be the most important study of the Pacific War ever published."
—*New Republic*

PACIFIC WAR

Saburo Ienaga, Pantheon, 0-394-73496-3, paper

"No one can really understand contemporary Japan and its policies unless he is acquainted with the grim story Saburo Ienaga presents."
—*New York Times Book Review*

UNFORGETTABLE FIRE

Japan Broadcasting Corporation, ed., Pantheon, 0-394-74823-9, paper

Over 100 vivid color drawings, and brief accompanying descriptions, by survivors of Hiroshima.

"More moving than any book of photographs of the horror could be."
—John Hersey

MEMOIRS FROM THE WAR IN EUROPE

THE WAR

Marguerite Duras, Pantheon Modern Writers, 0-394-75039-X, paper

"More than one woman's diary . . . a haunting portrait of a time and place and also a state of mind."
—*New York Times*

MEMOIRS 1925–1950

George Kennan, Pantheon, 0-394-71624-8, paper

"A remarkably candid, beautifully written and utterly fascinating autobiography."
—*New York Times*

NAPLES '44

Norman Lewis, Pantheon Modern Writers, 0-394-72300-7, paper

"A British officer's vivid, lucid, eloquent journal of a year in Allied-occupied Naples."
—*New York Times Book Review*

WAR DIARIES
Jean-Paul Sartre, Pantheon Modern Writers, 0-394-74422-5, paper

"An extraordinary book . . . His mental agility here is dazzling."   —Alfred Kazin

A WOMAN'S PRISON JOURNAL
Luise Rinser, Schocken, 0-8052-4045-4, cloth

At last available in America, Rinser's account of her year as a political prisoner in Nazi Germany was the first document of its kind published there after the war.

WORLD WAR II FICTION

THE BLOOD OF OTHERS
Simone de Beauvoir, Pantheon Modern Writers, 0-394-72411-9, paper

"One of the few books which depicts the atmosphere of Paris during its occupation."
—*New York Times*

THE ASSAULT
Harry Mulisch, Pantheon Modern Writers, 0-394-74420-9, paper

Probes the moral devastation following the Nazi's slaughter of an innocent family in retaliation for the assassination of a Dutch collaborator.

"A beautiful and powerful work . . . takes its place among the finest European fiction of our time."   —Elizabeth Hardwick

THE OGRE
Michel Tournier, Pantheon Modern Writers, 0-394-72407-0, paper

A riveting story of fascism and obsession.

"The most important book to come out of France since Proust."   —Janet Flanner

HOLOCAUST

UNANSWERED QUESTIONS
François Furet, ed., Schocken, 0-8052-0908-5, paper; 0-8052-4051-9, cloth

The first systematic investigation by an internationally acclaimed group of historians and scholars of the unanswered questions surrounding the Holocaust.
—*Just published*

CENTURY OF AMBIVALENCE
Zvi Gitelman, Schocken, 0-8052-4034-9, cloth

Nearly 400 rare photographs document Jewish life in the Soviet Union over the past century.

9 1 5 9 RABBINIC RESPONSA OF THE HOLOCAUST ERA
Robert Kirschner, Schocken, 0-8052-3978-2, paper

The religious life of Jews under Nazi rule from 1933 to 1945 is revealed in fourteen responses translated and presented in this unique anthology.